Designing Children's Creative Space

by
Seyed Sepehr Ershadi
Holder of Master's Degree in the filed of Architecture

Copyrights © 2023
All Rights Reserved for the Author

No part of this book may be reprinted or reproduced utilized in any electronic, mechanical or other means now known or here after invented, including photocopying and recording or any information storage or retrieval system, without permission in writing from the author. Moreover, the author keeps all the publication rights of this book for himself.

Title: Designing Children's Creative Space
Author: Seyed Sepehr Ershadi
Publisher: American Academic Research, USA
ISBN: 9781947464308

Dedicated to my dear parents

Table of Contents

Preface 13

Chapter 1. Generalities 15
   1.1 Introduction 16
   1.2 Objectives 19
   1.3 A History of Paying Attention to the Effect of Space Design on Creativity 20
   1.4 Methodology 26

Chapter 2. Literature and Theoretical Foundations of Creativity, Painting and Pre-School Education 27
   2.1 Introduction 28
   2.2 Theories of Creativity 28
   2.3 Creativity Constraints 32
      2.3.1 Family Obstacles and Restrictions to The Development of Creativity 33
   2.4 Signs and Symptoms of Creative People 35
   2.5 Creativity 35
      2.5.1 Definition of Creativity 35
      2.5.2 Personality Traits of Creative People 40
      2.5.3 Evolution of Creativity 42
      2.5.4 Creativity Training 44
         2.5.4.1 Training and research space 48
      2.5.5 Creativity and innovation 48
      2.5.6 Creative process 50
   2.6 History of the Subject 52
      2.6.1 An Overview of the History of Preschool Education 52
      2.6.2 The History of Creative Space for Children in England 53

2.6.3 The History of Creative Space for Children in Germany 53
2.6.4 The History of Creative Space for Children in Iran 54
2.7 Different Groups Using Kindergartens 55
2.8 Children's Activities in Preschool Age - Wants and Needs 55
    2.8.1 Educational Activities and Games for Toddlers 56
    2.8.2 Educational Activities and Games for Young Children 56
2.9 Developmental Psychology of Children 57
    2.9.1 Developmental Psychology of Children Under 6 Years Old 57
    2.9.2 Social Development of the Child 58
    2.9.3 Mental and Cognitive Development of the Child According to Piaget 59
    2.9.4 Child Development Stages in Preschool Period 60
2.10 Children and Playing 60
2.11 The Role of Play in Child Development 61
2.12 The Importance of Playing 61
2.13 Essential Tips for the Design of Play Equipment 62
2.14 Children's Painting 63
    2.14.1 Children and Painting 63
2.15 Child and Space 67
    2.15.1 Child and Architecture 67
        2.15.1.1 How to Design a Suitable Space for children 67
        2.15.1.2 Characteristics of a Suitable Space for Children 68
    2.15.2 Sensual and Intellectual Perception of Architectural Space 70
    2.15.3 Child and Forms 72
    2.15.4 Child and Natural Elements 73
    2.15.5 Symbols and Signs 73
    2.15.6 Child and Feelings 73
    2.15.7 Light and Color 74
    2.15.8 Dimensions and Sizes 75
    2.15.9 Child and Sounds 75
2.16 Child's Perception and attention to Space 76

2.17 Conclusion 77

Chapter 3. Data Analysis.. 79
   3.1 Reviewing Available Samples 80
      3.1.1 Domestic Samples of Iran 80
      3.1.2 Foreign Samples.. 94
   3.2 Conclusion 121
   3.3 Standards and Criteria for Kindergarten Architecture Design 124
      3.3.1 Interior Space Design Criteria.............................. 124
         3.3.1.1 Main Sections.. 124
         3.3.1.2 General Requirements................................. 124
      3.3.2 Administrative Department................................. 125
         3.3.2.1 Waiting Space 125
         3.3.2.2 Office Space 125
      3.3.3 Children's block 125
         3.3.3.1 Toddlers' block 125
         3.3.3.2 Young Children block.................................. 126
      3.3.4 Shared Spaces 128
         3.3.4.1 Multi-Purpose Hall....................................... 128
         3.3.4.2 Staircase 128
      3.3.5 Installation and Service Spaces............................ 129
         3.3.5.1 Kitchen.. 129
         3.3.5.2 Warehouse... 130
         3.3.5.3 Engine Room.. 130
      3.3.6 Playground 130
      3.3.7 Play Equipment... 131
         3.3.7.1 Merry-Go-Around 132
         3.3.7.2 Slide 132
         3.3.7.3 Swing 132
         3.3.7.4 Climbing frame 132
      3.3.8 Suggestions 132
      3.3.9 Criteria for Adapting Existing Buildings............. 133
         3.3.9.1 Criteria for Adaptation of Interior Spaces..... 133
      3.3.10 The Criteria for the Optimization of Open Space and Grounds 133

Chapter 4. Designing Children's Creative Space............. 135

4.1 Climatic Studies 136
  4.1.1 Geographical Characteristics of Tehran 136
  4.1.2 Natural Geographical Location of the Site 136
  4.1.3 Climatic Features 137
    4.1.3.1 Temperature 138
    4.1.3.2 Relative Humidity 138
    4.1.3.3 Rainfall Rate and Number of Rainy Days 138
    4.1.3.4 Freezing Days 139
    4.1.3.5 Snowy Days 139
    4.1.3.6 Wind 139
    4.1.3.7 Sunlight 140
4.2 Site 141
  4.2.1 Environmental Criteria for Kindergarten Location
.... 141
  4.2.2 Site Analysis 143
    4.2.2.1 Construction Density and Physical Texture of the Neighborhood 143
    4.2.2.2 Vehicle Traffic 144
    4.2.2.3 Neighboring Uses 144
    4.2.2.4 Accesses 145
    4.2.2.5 Checking the Entrances and Their Position on the Site 146
    4.2.2.6 Noise Pollution 147
    4.2.2.7 Climatic Conditions and Site 148
4.3 Key points 149
4.4 The Introduction of the Design Process 149
  4.4.1 Compilation of Keywords in Designing 149
  4.4.2 Physical Program 150
4.5 The Design Process 154
  4.5.1 Open Spaces 155
  4.5.2 Enclosed Spaces 156
    4.5.2.1 Kindergarten Classrooms 156
    4.5.2.2 Educational Classes 156
    4.5.2.3 Research Classes 158
    4.5.2.4 Workshop Classes 158
    4.5.2.5 Amphitheatre 158
    4.5.2.6 Administrative Block 159

- 4.5.3 Semi-Open Spaces 160
- 4.5.4 Installations 160
- 4.5.5 Structure 161
  - 4.5.5.1 Concrete Frame System 162
  - 4.5.5.2 The General Safety of Glasses 162
  - 4.5.5.3 Safety Requirements 163
- 4.6 Design Process Diagrams 164
- References 168

List of Figures

Figure 2-1 Diagram of different groups using kindergartens....55
Figure 3.1. Outdoor views of the kindergarten 81
Figure 3.2. Sand pools..82
Figure 3.3. Ball Pool 82
Figure 3.4. Colorology...83
Figure 3.5. Water and foam playing..83
Figure 3.6. Paint spraying 85
Figure 3.7. Training life skills...85
Figure 3.8. Gardening (planting flowers and plants) 86
Figure 3.9. Playing with water and foam 86
Figure 3.10. Using color and shapes in the facade....................87
Figure 3.11. Using colorful tree-like shapes on the wall, which has diversified the space 88
Figure 3.12. Children's playground 89
Figure 3.13 Various colors and artificial light in the kindergarten lobby 89
Figure 3.14. Color scheme and classroom furniture. 90
Figure 3.15. Kindergarten yard has green space, a gazebo, sandground, as well as a swimming pool which is under construction..91
Figure 3.16. Kindergarten playground......................................91
Figure 3.17. Children's creativity develops through space-making with wood, flowers and shells.......................................93
Figure 3.18. Wall Play Equipments 94
Figure 3.19. The training and play interior space of Barbapapà Kindergarten 94
Figure 3.20. Color and light in the interior space 95
Figure 3.21. Climatic design of the building............................96
Figure 3.22. Colored glass used in the building.......................96
Figure 3.23. Design of roof and lighting of the building 98
Figure 3.24. The building plan..98
Figure 3.25. Exterior facade of the kindergarten 8units............99
Figure 3.26. Exterior facade and children's play space............100
Figure 3.27. Dining hall – interior space.................................101

Figure 3.28. Plan and positioning of kindergarten 8units 102
Figure 3.29. Use of colors in the interior space - children's play space and part of the facade of the kindergarten 103
Figure 3.30. Some facades and sections of kindergarten 8units 103
Figure 3.31. CEBRA kindergarten design ideas 104
Figure 3.32. CEBRA kindergarten site plan 105
Figure 3.33. Exterior facade 106
Figure 3.34. Kindergarten plan 107
Figure 3.35. Exterior facade of Kierling Kindergarten 108
Figure 3.36. Use of glass and transparent materials and creating a break facade with the aim of increasing visual visibility to the natural environment 109
Figure 3.37. Use of maximum light for a group room 110
Figure 3.38. Linear organization of kindergarten space 111
Figure 3.39. Ground and first floor plan of the Kierling kindergarten 111
Figure 3.40. Trenten Kindergarten exterior facade 112
Figure 3.41. Positioning of the building 113
Figure 3.42. Integration of interior and exterior spaces through the interstitial space 114
Figure 3.43. Roof window used in the space between houses 115
Figure 3.44. Children's play space in Trenten Kindergarten ... 117
Figure 3.45. Kindergarten interior spaces 117
Figure 3.46. Facades and sections 118
Figure 3.47. Trenten Kindergarten plans 119
Figure 3.48. Building facade 119
Figure 3.49. Chicago kindergarten plan 121
Figure 3.50. Minimum height of staircase ceiling 129
Figure 3.51. Seats and staircase suitable for children's sizes .. 131
Figure 4.52 Site location 137
Figure 4.53 Wind 140
Figure 4.54 Sunlight 141
Figure 4.55 Detailed plan of the area 143
Figure 4.56 Municipality map (uses) of the site 145
Figure 4.57 Accesses of the desired site 146
Figure 4.58 Entrances of the site 147
Figure 4.59 Noise pollution of the site 147
Figure 4.60 Climatic conditions of the site 149
Table 4.1 Physical program 150
Figure 4.61 The diagram of Phase 1 164
Figure 4.62 The diagram of Phase 2 166

Figure 4.63 The diagram of Phase 3 166
Figure 4.64 The diagram of Phase 4 167

Preface

Due to the spread of scientific and technological events and their deep influence on all levels of life, today's world is called the world of communication and information. These d`iverse changes can be seen significantly in social, economic, and cultural fields. As one of the most basic concepts in the formation and development of the structure of a society, education has been strongly affected by this expansion. One of the important issues in today's world is the flourishing of creativity and innovation, on which the progress and development of countries depend. Competition, creativity, and innovation can be factors in winning in today's world. So, the mental creativity of children and adolescents should be nurtured and also flourished, effective factors in this field should be considered, and the foundations of creativity education should be promoted at the community level. Fostering creativity in childhood is effective throughout a person's life. Thus, it should be considered very important. According to Gardner, imagination formed in early childhood is the basis of creativity in adulthood. The correct education of children means providing the necessary preparations to actualize their abilities. It should help the emotional, physical, and intellectual development of children to easily deal with life's problems and conflicts and find solutions for them.

The acquired aspect of development and learning has been considered in many studies in the field of children. These studies have led to the emergence of various educational philosophies such as empiricism, naturalism, behaviorism, etc. According to new perspectives such as creative education, game-based learning is a process based on the child's creativity and initiative, which is formed under the influence of the physical and social environment. Creating spaces to host these learning methods seems necessary following designing them. The child-friendly public spaces, the open space movement, the development of open schools, multi-core schools, community schools, and the creation of museums, cultural centers, and children's parks are all responses to this need. According to studies, children's abilities and creativity are founded in childhood and the best time for the development of creativity and imagination is between 2 and 10 years of age, during which children are more influenced by the environment and are naturally curious about their environment.

Chapter 1.
Generalities

1.1 Introduction

Creativity is defined as production process, a person's innovation, high-quality and pure production (in an interpersonal and intra-individual process). Creativity is referred to as the ability to produce multiple, new, and suitable ideas and solutions to solve problems. Since innovation is the basis of creative power, the concept of the process, which is the development and cultivation of innovative ideas, should be emphasized in the development of children's creativity. As stated by Guilford, a distinction should be first made between convergent thinking and divergent thinking to understand the concept of the process. Convergent thinking problems often have a correct answer. However, divergent thinking problems require providing multiple new, innovative, high-quality, and executable solutions by the solver. Creativity should be distinguished from intelligence to achieve a correct understanding of children's creativity. Buildings are the physical reflection of various factors in urban spaces. Architecture has unique complexities because it is a cultural process that strongly affects the mentality of human societies. What is referred to as culture (rules, values, dos don'ts, etc.), is only a part of the culture of any society. Culture has another dimension called the material dimension, consisting of buildings, structures, and factories. These are also considered part of a society's culture because they are rooted in values and beliefs. This is where the link between culture and architecture appears. Preschool education has recently gained special importance due to the significant population of children in Iran.

So, the design of high-quality spaces must be given special attention. Unfortunately, most of the elementary schools and kindergartens in Iran are established in spaces without proper design or those with non-educational use (such as houses). Architectural principles are prepared for the design of educational spaces for 3–6-year-old children to improve their motivation and creativity. Children's creative spirit can be enhanced by changing or completing spaces and their components, interplaying open and closed spaces, and re-creating natural stimulus elements such as light, water, and plants. The design of educational spaces for children is of great importance because these places are the breeding ground for the future generation of the country. Many human abilities are developed during childhood. Besides, imagination and creativity are formed in childhood. Freud suggests that the source of creativity should be found in childhood experiences. Therefore, nurturing children's creativity should be considered in the early stages of their development. In a general approach, looking at creativity is associated with a development-oriented view and an effective orientation. Creativity has long been seen as an entirely innate, institutionalized, and almost inherited element. However, what is known today as creative attitude, creative design, creative talent, and most of all, creative thinking, is a paradigm beyond an element with an internal approach. In the new view of creativity, it is seen as education-oriented and development-oriented, and its strengthening and actualization are considered possible within the framework of intellectual affairs and practical fields. Experts define creativity as the ability to look at a subject in a new and different way, better and more organized understanding, guessing or organizing hypotheses, unconscious and guided perceptions leading to new insights, generating new and useful ideas, lateral thinking versus vertical thinking, divergent thinking versus convergent thinking, proposing new phenomena or methods and the ability to create using the power of imagination, providing new, unusual, and effective approaches, and making new connections. We consider creativity to be a person's imaginative and rational forces that break his/her mental patterns and intellectual limitations and provide new approaches to problem-solving using previous knowledge and discoveries. Man's reasoning and imagination powers are on both sides of his mental spectrum, and creativity is the product of the balanced and homogeneous cultivation of these two powers. The heterogeneous development of one of these two powers may make a person trapped in intellectual stagnation, fantasy, or melancholy. Creativity is based on imagination and reasoning, which together lead to the production of creative ideas. Creative people are generally those who have cultivated these two faculties well within them and use them for their purposes and goals. Many studies have been conducted recently on educational methods, the emotional and cognitive aspects of children, and educational issues, however, studies have often more focused on the effect of the quality of architectural space on the development of creativity. The design of special spaces for children such as kindergartens is important because the child's imagination becomes practical between the ages of 4 and 7. The child is more influenced by the environment during these years. Nevertheless, the spaces for children in Iran are not designed properly. Kindergartens are mainly located in residential spaces and even apartments, which are seemingly transformed into children's spaces by painting and coloring. We live in the world of colors and have become accustomed to colors to a great extent. One of the greatest blessings of God is the color of the world, which makes people happy and gives them hope and peace. Everyone is aware that colors exist, but do they know about their effect on their soul, mind, and thoughts? As psychologists say, colors have miraculous effects on people's souls and the interest in certain colors manifests many unsaid things in their minds and soul. In addition to colors, other factors can improve and develop children's creativity, such as green space, light, accessories, arrangement, what accessories and play equipment are made of, etc. All of these are examined in the study.

How can a space be designed for children so that their creativity flourishes?

The following seem to contribute significantly to the formation and development of a creative spirit in children:

1. Direct participation of children in the spatial arrangement of the kindergarten;
2. The intelligent entry of light into the space of a kindergarten;
3. Interior arrangement;
4. The use of happy colors suitable for the mood and age of children;
5. Designing green spaces in the kindergarten with appropriate dimensions.

1.2 Objectives

1. Achieving the principles of designing special spaces for children, emphasizing the use of environmental abilities that affect their minds and behavior;
2. Enhancing children's creative spirit through happy and entertaining spaces;
3. Designing the details of the space according to children's behavior patterns;
4. Promoting experiential motivation and evaluation skills in children;

5. Directing children to model the environment to be affected by the environment and have the necessary flexibility to make future decisions

1.3 A History of Paying Attention to the Effect of Space Design on Creativity

The concept of residence leads us to a method to influence it and the emotional and inherent roots of the residential space. Housing, in the general sense, is not just a residential unit but the entire residential environment. In other words, housing is more than just a physical shelter and covering all services and public facilities for human living. The house where the child grows up must have the characteristics of the world so that he/she can achieve full intellectual and mental development. In this study, the basics and principles of designing open spaces for residential complexes are defined. Since the open space is the place of occurrence of activities, the possibility of more diverse activities can be provided by creating desirable spaces that contribute to the vitality of the residential complex. The open spaces of residential complexes are designed to meet the needs of the residents or their users. So, the needs of the people in these spaces are first examined. 24-item questionnaires were designed to determine the solutions for the design of open spaces in residential complexes with the approach of promoting the creativity of children (3-12) in the open space, considering that creativity is affected by various components and variables. The questionnaires were then distributed among 36 child psychologists to check their reliability, and the results were analyzed. The reliability of the questionnaires was 0.7. This is a quantitative study, survey in terms of data collection method, and applied in terms of objectives. In this study, the correlation between the environmental quality of open spaces and children's health, physical development, and environmental creativity was investigated according to the needs, capabilities, and processes of physical and mental development of children and neighborhood and residential open spaces that affect the development and flourishing of their creativity. In this way, the features of the open space can lead to or hinder the emergence of creative abilities in children. The criteria of accessibility, scalability, attractiveness, competency, responsiveness, comfort, safety and participation are presented with an emphasis on the human attitude in design appropriate to children's development and creativity. The relationship between the factors of natural elements (plants, light, and water) and the factors of play participation, imagination, and curiosity are considered creative traits. The naturally stimulating elements promote children's curiosity and motivation for play and group participation, providing the basis for their imagination. In designing the open space of residential complexes, children's interaction with the daily life environment improves by establishing a balance between physical and psychological components. It promotes the child's interaction with the place in the open space of the residential complex. Piaget and Erikson argue that an environment can be created that has the characteristics of an appropriate emotional and physical environment by organizing space, time, and social contexts. Sufficient space for activities and available resources should be provided for children so that they can make the most of the experiences offered to them. Children cannot express themselves without access to resources, especially when trying to create 2D and 3D games. Following the international treaties and conventions that Iran has joined, children's enjoyment of citizenship rights today requires attention to their issues and their enjoyment of favorable living conditions, especially in urban and metropolitan areas. Nowadays, urban planners and practitioners pay special attention to child-friendly cities (CFC) because the number of children in the world's urban areas (cities in developing countries) is increasing. CFC projects mainly create opportunities for children to shape or change their environment. As members of society, children and adolescents are users of the artificial environment with a set of specific needs and desires. This study was conducted to design and plan the city for children, develop related guidelines, and provide criteria and standards for designing desirable living spaces for children in cities, especially metropolitan areas, to create a built environment that meets the psychological and physiological needs of children. In CFC, various sectors of society are committed to providing the necessary standards for children to live decently. In this city, the special needs and interests of children are considered. Accordingly, policies and programs called CFC have recently been proposed for the presence, development, and creative participation of children in urban spaces. Standards such as safety, security, access, beauty, adaptability, playability, training, participation, and financial facilities are important in CFC programs. So a space should be designed that provides the context for children's favorite activities in addition to fulfilling their expectations for the formation of a child-friendly place. It can be argued that the desirability of the child's space and the CFC is based on the interaction between the body, activity, and imagination, provided that these elements guarantee the increased quality of the child's landscape in the context of the cultural identity of the society while crystallizing the sense of freedom for the development of the child's creativity in the appropriate context of education and learning. One should sit in front of the magic box today to see the blossoming trees and go to the parks outside the city to hear the birds. Every day is the unmotivated repetition of the previous days, and the living environment is a platform for the repetition of common habits. Dormitory boxes without yards have made their way into our lives instead of lively houses with yards, ponds, and geraniums and the streets are all similar to each other with dictated views and drawn lines instead of winding and shadowy alleys with a stream in the middle. These spaces form people of today and tomorrow, many of whom are used to the previous day and do not try to recreate from it today. Their dynamism is lost in machine life, and there is not much room for the emergence of their creativity. It seems difficult to guide such people toward creative thinking and vision. The next generation will grow up in these spaces as well. So, creativity should be focused on in childhood by relying on the creative development of the next generation, because the spirit of exploration and the process of thinking and creativity in each person can be strengthened when this is provided to him/her from childhood. Accordingly, the environmental factors affecting children's creativity are explained by examining the role of the environment in its development. Children's understanding of the environment is recognized by reflecting on their daily lives. In this regard, efforts have been made to identify children's mentality of the physical space and record their mental image of the environment as well as their thought paths. A lot of data was collected through field investigation and direct encounters with children in different environments, part of which consists of interviews with children, questionnaires, and their movements and games, and another part consists of recording the child's mentalities through drawing. The success and progress of human beings depend on their fruitful and creative thoughts. The issue that has attracted the attention of researchers more than anything else in the era of increasing information and communication is how to grow and promote these fertile and creative thoughts. According to the findings of psychological science, childhood is the best time for training and flourishing human talents because all the acquired traits, behavior patterns, and necessary habits are obtained at this time and the child's real personality is formed accordingly. Among the many factors affecting the development of creativity of children, educational methods, emotional-cognitive aspects, as well as educational issues have been investigated recently, but less attention has been paid to the effect of the quality of the architectural space in fostering creativity. Meanwhile, studies suggest that the physical conditions of the environment affect the behavior of residents, the occurrence of normal and abnormal behaviors, and the promotion of creativity. According to Jon Lang, the change in the artificial environment will directly change behavior. So, children's personalities and behavior are affected by all the environments in which they are present. Meanwhile, educational spaces will be of special importance as one of the most important environments that affect a child's personality. As a cultural institute and educational aid, the Institute for the Intellectual Development of Children and Young Adults was established in 1965 to enrich free time and promote children's abilities and talents by producing and publishing books, films, and shows, creating bases for the supply of these products, and holding numerous educational classes. It continues to operate to date. The Institute for the Intellectual Development of Children and Young Adults is expected to play a bolder and more effective role in flourishing and promoting children's creativity and abilities, considering these lofty goals. However, experience indicates that the current functioning of this institute has moved away from its existential nature. In other words, it has become a one-dimensional institute that is limited to maintaining and filling children's free time instead of identifying and nurturing their talent and creativity. Since the quality of architectural space affects the development of creativity, one of the important reasons for the inefficiency of the Institute for the Intellectual Development of Children and Young Adults is its inefficient architecture. Like most educational spaces for children in Iran, this institute lacks a suitable design for children in such a way that most of their spaces are only office buildings that provide the basic needs of their users and seemingly have been turned into children's environments through paintings and coloring. They have also provided a stereotypical place for children instead of having diverse spaces, yards that offer nature to children, and workshops and dynamic classes that are designed for children and based on their needs. It seems difficult to guide children who experience being in such an environment toward creative thinking and vision because the spirit of exploration and the process of thinking and creativity in each person can be strengthened when this is provided to them from childhood. However, an institute can be built that provides the basis for the flourishing and development of children's creativity in addition to fulfilling social goals by recognizing and relying on the capabilities of the Institute for the Intellectual Development of Children and Young Adults and applying the principles that promote creativity in the design of special spaces for children. School is a social institution where students learn how to look at the world, life skills, and knowledge and get to know the habits and customs of society. The elements constituting the educational space in which the students attend should be a set in which they feel belong to the place. Education is realized in a dynamic and flexible architectural environment. Every child has an impulse to create that is ready to be realized, but it is up to us to create the conditions to support children's creative efforts. The main subject of the study is the impact of creativity on architecture, and the practical subject is the design of a girls' primary school according to the study's achievements, including the design of spaces for children based on their needs and expectations of the environment, characteristics affecting the development of children's creativity, children's level of cognitive development, children's perception and the mental image of the environment, how children deal with the environment, understanding the effect of architectural space on arousing children's sense of belonging to the environment, and creative thinking in children. This is a qualitative study, the goal of which is to produce creativity that can crystallize in all respects. Providing peace and mental security is the first environmental condition for a child that can be the basis of creativity. The environment must be responsive to the conflicting needs of children. In such an environment, motivation and driving factors must interact with peace and tranquility, and risk-taking must oppose security. According to the results, psychological freedom for creative thinking occurs when there is a sense of belonging to a place and peace, and these two opposite things are complementary.

1.4 Methodology

The method used in this book is descriptive-analytical. The purpose of the researcher is to describe and explain the how and why of the problem and its dimensions, in addition to illustrating what it is. To explain and justify the reasons, the researcher needs solid reasoning foundations that are provided through reviewing the literature and theoretical discussions and developing general propositions and theorems about it. The researcher logically connects the details of the problem with the relevant general propositions and concludes. In descriptive studies, the researcher does not interfere in the status and role of the variables, does not manipulate or control them and only studies and describes what exists. General findings and theorems can be obtained in descriptive studies in another way, that is, using the inductive method. In this method, comments can be made based on common characteristics or attributes between various phenomena and objects and their repetition.

Chapter 2.
Literature and Theoretical Foundations of Creativity, Painting and Pre-School Education

2.1 Introduction

When it comes to talk about ways of nurturing creativity, what promptly comes to our mind is fighting with the role of disincentives. In this case, one should consider strengthening creativity versus removing disincentives as the first step towards nurturing creativity. In the real world, the role of factors that help delay or damage creativity is very significant, and this is while creativity seeks a suitable platform for its growth and development. There are deterrent factors of creativity that can cause it to be stopped and silenced forever. By accepting the fact that creativity is affected by the traumatic factors, the role of deterrent factors become significant, and accordingly, investigating the role of these factors can help the process of stimulating and re-invigorating the creativity under the title of "acceleration". Recognition of the barriers on one hand helps understand the harm caused by creativity, and on the other hand, helps design and determine suitable and alternative patterns in order to remove the barriers. The aim of introducing the deterrent factors in this section is to clarify the effect of each of them on the cycle of growth and evolution of creativity.

2.2 Theories of Creativity

Creativity-related theories: now let's look at the views related to creativity. A theory is usually an opinion and knowledge that explains a phenomenon. Each view raises a specific knowledge of a subject or concept, so when we talk about the perspectives, we mean ideas that are not similar to each other, i.e., any view raises a new perspective.

1. Theory of divine spirit: According to an ancient theory, creativity descends from God to man and does not have a worldwide distribution. So some people get more shares than others do and thus, creative people are more dependent on the source of grace. However, when scientific thinking becomes dominant, this theory of creativity is inappropriate and there is a need to seek more convincing evidence.

2. Psychoanalytical view: According to this view, creativity is referred to the conflict existing in our unconscious mind or nature. Our unconscious mind tries to find a solution to the conflict, and if the solution is compatible with the conscious part or the self, it can be considered as a creative solution. But if it is in conflict with our conscious part, it causes mental illness. Therefore, from the psychoanalysis view, creativity and mental illness originate from the source, but the difference is that a creative person has reasonable control over his/her unconscious, while one with a mental illness is suffering from extreme dissipation.

Those with mental illness behave in an extreme manner in controlling their unconscious behavior. With too much control, behavior becomes stereotyped, and by letting go of control, behavior becomes uncontrollable. In the second case, the person often experiences hallucinations and dreams.

In psychoanalytic therapy, the patient is helped to release his/her "self" without showing his/her unconscious anxiety, and thus with voluntary control of his/her creative power. Freud believed that creativity can be considered especially as an alternative capability to a childhood game, an attempt to solve the unconscious, which is due to childhood experiences; in other words, in this way, the needs in a child's head are manifested as work and art. He also believed that new ideas spring from conflict and are a defense mechanism, but in reality, creativity is also a defensive action, and artistic and practical activities cannot meet the needs of higher goals. So, one tries to be creative in order to satisfy certain drives as well as to restore the balance disturbed by the drives. Theories of the psychoanalytic school of thought about creativity can be interpreted in several ways, as Freud believed that creativity is a defensive behavior to reduce stress, and although creativity tries to reduce stress, it is an end in itself.

Behaviorism perspective: Although behaviorists' or communication theorists' view of creativity does not have enough breadth and depth, behavioral experts have tried not to fall behind in explaining creativity, and have drawn their attention to a few points that we will briefly address here: From communication theorists' point of view, creativity is a link between thoughts, which follows the principles of "freshness", "clarity" and "abundance". For example, clearer, more refreshing, and more repetitive communication will lead the person to be more creative. In behavioral terms, creativity can be defined as a behavior based on unique and new patterns.

Psychometric perspective: The psychometric perspective, which plays an important role in the growth and initiation of creativity, refers to the analysis of the factors and elements of creativity, which actually explains the basic structure of creativity in a measurable and scientific way. Guilford is one of the initiators of this view and, in fact, the development of creativity is due to his efforts. He believes that people are different in how they are sensitive to the problem. For example, consider two scientists who intend to prepare a scientific report. According to Guilford, only one of these two scientists can refer to the problem in his scientific report. The scientist who is more sensitive to the problem can achieve specific results and even solve the problem creatively, while if the second scientist does not hear about the problem, he will not be able to solve it and therefore, would not support it; so he would not have a chance for creative thinking. Guilford also believes that people differ in how easily they come up with ideas. He considers two main skills as involving creativity: divergent thinking and convergent thinking. According to him, divergent thinking is mainly defined as fluidity, adaptability, change, and expansion, while divergent thinking is characterized by the fact that it lacks the processes and characteristics of logical and natural thought and is similar to the first train of thought in Freudian Theory. The main advantage is "Freedom from contracts." Divergent thinking is drawn to the unknown and unfamiliar and is risky and skeptical as well. This type of thinking can lead to many solutions when examining a problem. In fact, in everyday life, a person is constantly involved in divergent thinking in order to find a different answer, e.g., consider someone who is left behind the door due to forgetting the key is likely to go through the possible solutions with his mind. In order to open the door; however, he ultimately would seek an answer that is appropriate and true for the situation. Convergent thinking is therefore conservative and based on methods and rules. This type of thinking can turn new thoughts into old ones, but it cannot introduce new patterns. Rather, it monitors the progress of divergent thinking. In other words, convergent thinking uses information for "elimination", just as in the case one uses logic in order to arrive at the correct answer out of different information.

Humanistic view: This view is regarded among the schools of thought with a strong focus on creativity. Humanists do not attribute creativity solely to unusual things, believing that everyone can benefit from his/her creative power. They believe that creativity accounts for not only results but also activities, processes, and relationships. As Rogers says in his definition of creativity: The emergence of a new communicational result in science originates on the one hand from singularity and, on the other hand, from matters of events, humans, and their living conditions based on humanists' views. The internal conditions of creativity cannot be imposed just as a planted seed cannot be forced to grow. Humanists pay particular attention to the relationship between creativity and mental health, self-actualization and human flourishing. This relationship is so deep that it can be said that these words have united meaning. Humanists believe that the possibility of evidence lies within each individual and by giving freedom to people, society should give them the opportunity to experience and act so that creativity flourishes in them. In this way, any limitation or assessment imposed by the environment is an obstacle to creativity.

2.3 Creativity Constraints

Creativity emerges as a divine and all-encompassing gift that requires the development of a suitable platform for growth and development. Therefore, to develop this capability, barriers and factors must be explored. Different factors throughout life affect the development of creativity in different ways, from birth to adulthood, and play the role of obstacle and problem. In this regard, various classifications have been proposed by experts. Here we discuss a form of classification of the obstacles to growth of creativity and explain some cases.

Obstacles and Constraints of Creativity Development

1. a) Family; b) Cultural barriers and educational environment; and c) Society;

2. Individual, psychological;

3. Historical;

4. Physiological; and

5. Biological.

• Social barriers and restrictions: Each society has certain customs and traditions and differs from other societies in a variety of social activities, interests, and behaviors. All members of a society often assume that they break the rules, then they have done an illegal behavior, and will punish and eject anyone who tries to break the accepted patterns. Therefore, a creative behavior is sometimes considered as destructive in society and endangers a person's stability and a person of importance.

2.3.1 Family Obstacles and Restrictions to The Development of Creativity

Many parents are unaware that their children will not become what they want, but they will become what they are. So, due to their compassion and concern for their children's future, they adopt methods and models to deal with their children, which unfortunately contradicts the parents' intentions and wishes.

• Parents' lack of familiarity with the true concept of creativity: In Some parents, the lack of knowledge and understanding about the process of developing their children's creativity leads to a lack of creativity development. Parents have similar perceptions of various qualities such as intelligence, memory, talent, and creativity, but they are less successful in developing their children's conscious creative thinking.

• Implementation of hard and cumbersome rules at home: inflexible rules and regulations, dos and don'ts, commands and prohibitions, like "do this ..., if ..., but, ..." would go against the development of children's creativity in their family.

• Constant criticism of behavior: Sometimes checking and criticizing a child's behavior by family increases his/her fear of mistakes and failure, and if this fear turns into an illness, it can even prevent him/her from doing new things.

• Ignoring a child's imagination: Children's imagination, the growth peak of which occurs at the age of 5 years, is a sense of creativity, and considering it useless and accusing the child of lying, which is considered as one of the natural characteristics of imaginative children at the age of 4 to 6 years, dries up the source of creativity in children.

•Failure to discover the child's ability, talent and inner interests: due to parents' ignorance of their child's abilities, which can provide the basis for its emergence and growth at different ages, it leads to the lack of recognition and lack of discovery and non-fertilization of what is institutionalized in a person's existence. part of which will be the lack of creativity.

• Lack of humor in the family.

• Creating competition among children.

• Family's efforts in their child's pre-puberty phase to eliminate his/her fantasies.

Until a child is not developed mentally, physically, and emotionally, he/she cannot be given the necessary training. As a result, nurturing precedes education. The game plays an important role for child's thinking. Children at preschool age learn through play and facing and adapt to their surrounding environment. A good relationship with a child can be established through playing with him/her. In this way, he starts to know his/her inner self and discover his/her abilities. The development of the child's nervous, behavioral, and personal characteristics is simple at first, then it will become progressive and systematic, and advanced. Even if there are some obstacles during the child's growth period, if these steps are taken late, they would not lead to his/her overall retardation.

2.4 Signs and Symptoms of Creative People

The main characteristics of a creative person include: honesty with him/herself and self-organization, humor and frankness, commitment and order, altruism and simplicity of behavior, high tolerance threshold, coping power, wide interests, desire to change, perseverance and seriousness.

2.5 Creativity

One of the cognitive traits that has attracted researchers' attention in various fields, e.g., entrepreneurship, is "creativity". Given the variety of problems humans face in today's world, it is particularly important to consider the issue of creativity.

2.5.1 Definition of Creativity

In today's world, the promotion of creativity is regarded as one of the fundamental axes of the educational system, so that teachers encourage their students to develop or limit their creativity by teaching them to think creatively and promote their abilities. Indeed, creativity is not a fixed characteristic that is present in a human's life without changes or transformations, but it is enhanced or weakened by the influence of factors or obstacles. Therefore, giving special attention to the development of creative abilities in children and students at an early age is considered as one of the most important issues that education experts have always observed and advised. Humans need to cherish children's creativity in order to survive. Creativity, like intelligence, memory and thought, is a dynamic subject that can be learned, developed and strengthened in various ways.

There are different definitions of creativity; for example: asking questions; solving problems by looking ahead to obtain innovative solutions adapted to each area; having two main features: motivation and need ; new and reinforcing perspectives or behaviors arising from the relationship between one's thinking and sociocultural background; the process of raising awareness of problems, gaps, knowledge gaps, contradictions, etc.; defining the problem, looking for a solution, guessing hypotheses; formulating and testing hypotheses; and finally communicating the results. Most psychologists also agree that creativity refers to new and valuable achievements of high quality.

Creativity consists of three basic areas: skill, experience, and motivation. The skill area refers to a talent in a certain area and is partially inherent. The expertise area means that no matter how talented someone is, he/she cannot create creative works without sufficient experience. People also have various motivational qualities, e.g., a strong desire to succeed and commitment to the field they have chosen for their work.

Sternberg (1988) addresses the need to see creativity as a multidimensional quality in his interactive theory and states that divergent thinking is only a part of creativity, not its whole, considers creativity as a multifaceted phenomenon and says that creativity is the result of three dimensions of intelligence, stylistics, and motivation, and the combination of these dimensions causes people to act creatively or non-creatively in their thinking and acting. One of the most important conditions and methods for making creativity flourish is to provide an atmosphere that is inspiring, flexible and generally creative. In turn, in addition to preparing such an environment in schools, teachers need to provide students with the necessary background and the desired environment. Creative kids need creative teachers, and an inquiring classroom encourages creativity. When teachers and students ask problematic questions, they find new solutions to problems, and students are involved in the development of new ideas and discovery of new and innovative results. Creativity not only gives the child satisfaction, but also gives him/her self-confidence and allows him/her to involve with the outside world. To encourage creativity in students, schools need to provide flexible curricula and use teaching methods that encourage divergent thinking, as the use of these methods, in addition to stimulating creative thinking, also creates problems for creative students and stimulates them to solve the problems. By encouraging children to solve their problems, teachers and parents improve their creative output. Teachers, in the position of providing the learning conditions of students, are responsible for creative education and fostering creativity in students through innovation, flexibility, not forcing students to memorize and accumulate mentally, humor, avoiding formal strategies and methods of education, laying the groundwork for students' self-expression, and increasing their self-confidence. Different theorists have proposed different definitions for creativity. In the book titled "The Blackwell Dictionary of Cognitive Psychology", creativity is defined as the ability to find unconventional and high quality solutions for problems (Eysenck, 1994). Warren (1934) describes creativity as an ability and talent in some people for making new compositions and works in the fields of art, mechanics, etc., which were previously unknown. Stein (1962) considers creativity as the creation of new work that is embraced by a large group as something that can be championed or enjoyed in its time.

According to Eysenck (1979), creativity is the ability to see new connections, realize unusual ideas, and break out of traditional thinking patterns.

Torrance (1998) suggests three definitions of creativity in three areas: research, artistic and related to survival. According to him, the research definition of creativity is the process of sensing problems, issues, gaps in information, missing elements, awkward things, guessing and hypothesizing about these flaws and evaluating and testing these guesses and hypotheses, revising and testing them again, and finally, communicating the results. According to Torrance, the cause of creative work is an attempt to release a feeling of stress – a feeling of tension arising from a defect or deficiency. In his artistic definition of creativity, Torrance gives a few examples: Creativity is like trying to find out; looking back; eliminating mistakes; and reading in your own style. In his survival-dependent definition of creativity, Torrance considers creativity as the ability to cope with difficult and dangerous situations when a person has no pre-learned and practice. Robert Gagne (1985) considers creativity as a type of problem solving, in terms of the relationship between creativity and problem solving, he states: every scientific discovery or great artistic work is surely a result of problem solving activity.

It is true that sometimes a solution to a problem comes to thinkers' minds in the form of "insight", but they may have considered this issue in their thoughts for some time. As a problem-solving behavior, these creative acts are based on a large level of previously discovered knowledge, either of the "general" type known in the sciences, or of the "specific" type known to the artist. Despite this, it must be accepted that when solving a problem, a person is faced with a situation where he/she has to find an answer to a question or problem, while in creativity, a creative person considers both the question and its answer. However, the novelty of outcomes is a result of creative thinking. According to Woolfolk (1987), the main core of all concepts related to the semi-conscious is involved in solving the problem, so that the person does not think about solving the problem consciously and with prior planning, but he/she freely combines new information with his/her past thoughts and finds a kind of reorganization.

A. Sternberg's and Davidson's points of view:

This method, with a more empirical basis than Wallace's method, was proposed by Sternberg and Davidson (1983) and consists of 3 steps.

1- Selective encryption

Selective encryption involves identification of the necessary information among all the available information.

2- Optional combination

Selective combination involves knowing how to put together the relevant information.

3- Selective comparison

Selective comparison involves relating to information about the current problem to the relevant information that has already been obtained.

B. View of creative cognition:

According to this theory, creativity is a mental phenomenon that originates from the use of normal cognitive processes. Proponents of this view believe that just as laboratory experiments have provided insight into human cognition, the same methodology can be used to study creative thinking. Laboratory studies show that visual mental images can play an effective role in the formation of creative thinking. Since an optimal activity associated with creativity requires normal cognitive processes, creative thinking is achievable for almost everyone.

C. View of Expertise Acquisition:

Some studies have shown that exceptional talents are largely acquisitive rather than intrinsic. These talents cover a wide range of activities, from competitive sports like chess to working and mastering a musical field. Based on this, evidence shows that creativity also requires a significant level of training and practice. Even a creative genius cannot escape this inherently difficult path of discipleship. From this point of view, it can be said that people do not initially generate creative thoughts, but this type of thinking arises from a large amount of information that they have already obtained. Accordingly, it can be said that people are equal in terms of their ability to achieve creativity.

2.5.2 Personality Traits of Creative People

Considering the effect that creative people can have in producing and presenting new thoughts and ideas, paying attention to their characteristics is of particular importance. The most important characteristics mentioned by different researchers include: high intelligence, high self-confidence, high information and awareness, cheerfulness, curiosity, skepticism and pessimism. For example, Taylor (1966) considers the following characteristics for creative people: cheerfulness, wit, curiosity, search, ability to reproduce ideas, autonomy and independence. Also, Stein (1974) considers high progress, motivation, great curiosity, unconventional personality, independence, critical thinking and perseverance among these characteristics. In other cases, some characteristics are mentioned that prevent the emergence of creativity, e.g., dominance, negativity, fear, fault-finding, compromise, submission to power, shyness.

Although among the characteristics mentioned for creative people, more attention has been paid to their "intelligence" by researchers. Research shows that a certain level of intelligence is necessary for the expression of creative behavior, but beyond that, intelligence has little to do with creative behavior. In general, the results of various surveys do not show any significant correlation between intelligence tests and the results of tools measuring creativity. For example, Torrance (1975) reviewed 187 studies that examined the relationship between creativity and intelligence, with the result that the correlation coefficient between the results of intelligence and creativity tests is 0.20. It is assumed that the reason for the low correlation coefficient between intelligence and creativity lies in the high homogeneity in the subjects, so that when the correlation coefficient of intelligence and creativity in the subjects whose intelligence is above 120 is calculated, this coefficient is very low, but when the subjects are selected inhomogeneous include all the subjects with different intelligence gains, the correlation coefficient between intelligence and creativity becomes more significant. Therefore, it can be concluded that intelligence tests alone are not a good way to identify creative children. In addition to this, another reason for the low correlation between intelligence and creativity in intelligence tests may be related to the concept of intelligence, because in this type of research, the one-dimensional concept of intelligence is used. While multi-dimensional theories of intelligence can better show the relationship between certain dimensions of intelligence and creativity. An example is Raymond Kettle: Fluid intelligence and crystallized intelligence. Fluid intelligence refers to the ability or talent to acquire new knowledge and solve new problems. Crystallized intelligence means the accumulation of knowledge throughout life and the application of previous knowledge in solving problems. In this area, fluid intelligence is more related to creativity. Similarly, Guilford (1967) presents a model of intelligence which includes three levels of functioning, content and product, each of which is subdivided into sub-levels. Guilford offers two types of thinking in the science part, i.e., convergent and divergent thinking. In convergent thinking, it is important to arrive at one acceptable answer, so that the answers and solutions are predictable and have a clear, predetermined structure. While divergent thinking involves multiple responses and lacks clear and predictable solutions to the problem. Fluency (generating a certain number of thoughts at a certain time), flexibility (creating diverse and unusual ideas and different solutions to solve a problem) and freshness or originality (using unique and novel solutions) are among the characteristics of divergent thinking. Thus, it can be concluded that divergent thinking is closely related to creativity.

2.5.3 Evolution of Creativity

Creativity is a behavior that develops throughout one's life. According to researchers, changes and transformations in creative activities can be results of different factors at different stages of life. Some of these factors are familial, some social, and some educational. Several family-related factors such as birth order, presence and absence of parents, and parenting methods are mentioned as effective factors for change and evolution of creativity. For example, families of creative people do not complain about financial problems as often as families of people with high intelligence. In families of creative people, mothers are more employed, do not see undesirable qualities in their children, and are more dissatisfied with their parenting methods. Potential creativity apparently requires that a person be exposed to various experiences that weaken the constraints imposed by society. He/she should also have stimulating experiences that help his/her stability. In other words, it can be said that some of the most harmful childhoods are likely to become the most creative adults. The social contexts that are effective for evolution, growth and development of creativity include the interpersonal environment, the environment related to the scientific field, and the social and cultural environment.

Interpersonal environment: This environment contains one's expectations for displaying creative behavior. Research shows that rewarding students increases their creative behavior (Sternberg, 1988). Interpersonal expectations are also important in teaching creativity, especially using the brainstorming method. In the talk about teaching creativity, we will discuss brainstorming as well.

The environment related to a creative scientific discipline does not change in a vacuum, but creative behavior emerges in interaction with other people, as well as a scientific, artistic or literary discipline. Three parts of the system interact to generate creative behavior:

1) a creative person; 2) a discipline or a field of expertise that is composed of a set of rules, a treasure of techniques and any other abstract feature that defines a certain state of creativity; and 3) Colleagues, i.e., people who work in a similar field of expertise. By accepting these three subsystems, we will implicitly accept that it is very difficult to study creativity with common psychological methods. Thus, study of creative behavior should be done based on the scientific field. Special methods have been proposed to achieve these goals, including the use of archival data to study the interaction between creative people and their scientific fields, and following up the participant. Although these methods are effortful, the

information resulting from these methods cannot be achieved in any other way.

Socio-cultural environment: As mentioned in the section on the effects of the environment related to the academic field of the development of creativity, the work environment and interaction with peers play an effective role in generating creativity. At a broader level, sociocultural factors can play a significant role in the development of creativity. Among the social factors negatively affecting creativity is an unsafe and chaotic social environment, so that living in a turbulent social and political environment with killings and coups is not consistent with the growth of creativity. On the other hand, they lead a peaceful life where different groups can live together in peace. On the other hand, living in a peaceful environment where different groups live together peacefully can lead to the flourishing of creativity. Also, societies and cultures that openly accept new and different ideas and allow people to make diverse choices provide the basis for the emergence of creativity.

2.5.4 Creativity Training

Given the variability of intelligence, there may still be ambiguities and disagreements, and also there are those who consider intelligence as an unreachable characteristic. But all nurturing psychologists and specialists believe that the capability of creativity and divergent thinking can be taught, especially to children and teenagers. In order to teach creativity, two axes are usually considered.

A. Factors fostering creativity at school

If we believe that there are particular factors at school that promote the development and fertility of creativity, by taking a few hints we can change the school environment so that creativity can grow and flourish. Some of the suggestions in this regard are as follows.

1- Strengthening students' creative behavior

Research shows that students' creative activities increase when they receive rewards (Sternberg, 1988). Students' innovative work and imagination should be encouraged in order to strengthen their divergent thinking. Also, asking questions starting with why and how that can have multiple answers can increase students' creativity and divergent thinking.

2. Use of model-building methods to teach creativity.

The model-building and observation methods are among the most effective methods for teaching creativity. Some research has shown that students who had a creative role model showed more creative behavior compared to those who did not have a creative role model. This indicates that model-building teaching methods lead to more creative behaviors in university students than traditional teaching methods do.

3. Respecting students' individual differences

Each student has his/her own specific ability, so teachers should avoid forcing them to compete. The results of some studies show that if teachers deal with their students in the right way, this will have a major impact on the growth and development of creative skills in them. For example, by evaluating the educational status of 400 students in the 20th century, it is concluded that they were more interested in teachers who had allowed them to progress according to their abilities, gave them the opportunity to work in preferred subjects and encouraged them to think.

4. Providing students with opportunities for self-directed and inquiry-based learning.

One of the characteristics of creative people is their personal independence and their ability to find solutions to problems through discovery and self-learning. Thus, teachers should make students interested in the use of original solutions and creative activities. Some researchers believe that students' creativity should be given more credit.

5. Pay attention to factors that impede the student's creativity

Sometimes the formal and disciplined environment of the school binds the student to strictly follow the school rules, which in turn can prevent their exploratory activities and imaginative play. On the other hand, it is possible, imaginations and thoughts stimulated by these games, which sometimes seem "irrelevant", can provide a basis for creativity. If students ask "irrelevant" questions, the best way is to follow such questions with their own content and ask them to think more about the issue. When a student evaluates their thinking, they are less likely to avoid questions in the future.

In order to provide the condition for flourishing and emergence of students' creativity, Torrance (1962) proposes principles, including:

1. Make children more sensitive to environmental stimuli.

2. Encourage children to work with objects and ideas.

3. Help children tolerate new and innovative ideas.

4. Teach children to use constructive criticism.

5. Encourage active and self-initiated learning.

6- Create needs for the emergence of creativity.

B. Specific methods and techniques for teaching creativity.

Some methods and techniques have been suggested for teaching creativity in people, the most important of which include brainstorming, Gordon technique, and teaching research skills.

1. Brainstorming method

The brainstorming method is the most famous creativity training method proposed by Osborn (1957). In this method, persons are given a problem and asked to express as many solutions as they can think of to solve the problem. Before presenting all the solutions, no judgment and evaluation are presented about the opinions presented. But before presenting the solutions, they are told that more frequent, fresh and usable solutions will get more points. brainstorming has the following principles:

A. Late judgment: Any kind of evaluation and criticism of ideas is prohibited in order to allow the emergence of new ideas.

B. Changing or combining ideas is encouraged.

C. More and more ideas and solutions are requested.

D. Presentation of unconventional, unreasonable and far-reaching ideas is encouraged.

2. Gordon technique

This technique (1961), is similar to the brainstorming method, with the difference that in the brainstorming method, people are given a complete and detailed problem and are asked to provide solutions, while in Gordon's technique, people are given an abstract of a problem. This is because Gordon believes that proposing a problem in an abstract way leads to the presentation of ideas and solutions. For example, for parking cars in a place. But in brainstorming method, people are asked to express different ways to store and accumulate things.

3. Research skills method

In this method, students are taught the methods of hypothesis design and hypothesis testing so that, when encountering problems, they can hypothesize their solutions, collect and summarize the information needed to test hypotheses, and choose the best hypothesis. The higher number of hypotheses a person makes, the more likely they are to find a satisfactory answer.

2.5.4.1 Training and research space

From a lexical point of view, training refers to education and everything related to education and nurturing. Terminologically, educational space refers to all buildings that are related to educational issues in some way, including classroom buildings – administrative area, sports area, educational buildings – amphitheater, etc.

2.5.5 Creativity and innovation

Nowadays, creativity and innovation have become very important in different fields, as today's world is known as a world of knowledge and information, and in all sectors where knowledge is considered important, creativity and innovation can add value to existing knowledge. Firestein (1996) mentioned creativity and innovation as necessary strategic tools for any organization and business.

In today's world that is characterized by rapid change and intensive competition, creativity is not only the most important source of competitive profit, but also essential for human survival. Also, there is an entrepreneurship system in creativity. Entrepreneurs approach their problems creatively and often feel the need to express new visions and ideals. Creativity is important for entrepreneurs because they have many tools such as people, capital, market, ideas and thoughts, and so they need to organize these tools in new and different ways to success. Thus, creativity is considered as one of the necessary conditions for the organization in its operational process. Creativity is, therefore, one of the necessary prerequisites for successful entrepreneurial activities.

Relationship between creativity and motivation

Before discussing the relationship between creativity and motivation, it is necessary to mention two types of motivations in humans. Motivations are generally divided into groups: Intrinsic and extrinsic.

Intrinsic motivation refers to the desire to do something for its own sake, because it is attractive, fun, and satisfying in itself and brings positive challenges. Extrinsic motivation refers to the desire to work to achieve an external goal, regardless of the work itself.

What can you do?

What do you want to do?

How would you like to work?

What is meant by qualifications is:

- You have expertise in the field.

- You have acquired the necessary technical skills.

- You have talent and skills.

- You have a cognitive approach combined with flexibility.

- You have an active work style and stability.

- You have a tendency to take risk-taking and independence.

When employees have strong internal motivation, their performance is good. Thus, creative people are primarily motivated by automatic interest, joy and satisfaction, not by external pressure.

2.5.6 Creative process

Although new ideas spontaneously come to our mind, they are actually the result of a creative process that includes the following 7 steps:

Preparation: In this step, the person prepares his/her mind for creative thinking. Preparation can include formal education, internships, work experience, and other learning opportunities. These trainings lead to the development of a framework for creativity and innovation.

Investigation: People can gain insight into problems or solutions through research and study. In order to generate new ideas and concepts in a given field, one must first find a problem and identify its main points.

Transformation: This step includes identification of the similarities and differences in the collected data. This activity requires two types of thinking: convergent and divergent. Convergent thinking involves the ability to see similarities and connections between different pieces of information and events, while divergent thinking refers to the ability to see the differences between different information and events.

Incubation period: The human subconscious needs time to reflect the information gathered. For an observer, this stage of the creativity process can be very frustrating because nothing appears to be happening. In fact, during this stage it seems that the creative person is wasting his/her time.

Breakthrough: In a sense, this stage happens during the incubation period. If a significant increase occurs accidentally, this stage may occur after 5 minutes or 5 years. In the breakthrough stage, all of the previous stages come together in order to bring about the "I have found" moment.

Verification: For entrepreneurs, validating an idea as a valid and usable idea can involve bringing the product or service to market, small pilot projects, testing prototypes, or other activities in order to find out whether the new idea is viable and can be implemented or not.

Implementation: Many people have creative ideas for developing new products or services, but these ideas are never materialized; i.e., the idea cannot come true. This is what distinguishes entrepreneurs from others. Entrepreneurs have a philosophy: prepare, target and shoot, don't prepare, targeting, targeting, targeting, and so on.

Can creativity be taught? In the distant past, it was generally believed that people were either creative or not. But today we have a better understanding of creativity. Research shows that everyone has the opportunity to become a creative person through learning. Everyone has the potential to be creative, and creativity is not an exclusive trait of a very small group of people.

The biggest problem is that most organizations do not teach their employees to become creative. People are constrained by traditional ideologies and most of them never use their natural creativity

2.6 History of the Subject

2.6.1 An Overview of the History of Preschool Education

Education and care of children are as old as human history. However, child care centers operated widely with industrial development, the rise of women's role in society, and their presence in all social arenas. These centers initially paid less attention to the educational aspects of children and only took care of them at certain hours in exchange for money. Kindergartens came into being in their current form and took on part of the responsibility of raising and educating children under 6 years of age with the development and progress of societies and the growing need for a safe environment that both takes care of children and improves their awareness and knowledge. These centers took initial steps to develop children's personalities and improve their skills, in addition to familiarizing them with values, creating social relationships, and developing them.

In the past few decades and with the beginning of living in apartments, limited and closed spaces, and children's lack of access to the necessary spaces to play with their peers and active games such as running, jumping, etc., these centers have become more important.

Developed countries have been conducting many studies on child care and education for about 70 years. Besides, about 80 to 95% of children in these countries benefit from this education with government support.

2.6.2 The History of Creative Space for Children in England

Child care centers were founded in 1816 in New Lanark, Scotland, by Robert Owen. He opened these centers for the children of his mill workers. In this center, children were introduced to some social principles while playing, singing, listening to folk stories, and doing rhythmic activities. The development of this activity lasted slowly until 1911 when Margaret McMillan and her sister Rachel realized the educational role and importance of the family and began to educate the family for the first time. McMillan was one of the first people who saw the need for continuous and in-service training for teachers and managers so that they could respond to the growing and changing needs of children by updating their awareness.

Margaret McMillan's efforts greatly influenced preschool education in England, leading to the approval of the Fisher Act in 1918. In this way, kindergartens were officially approved and developed throughout England. In these kindergartens, children are taught basic life skills, familiarity with nature, self-care in maintaining health, developing their senses, developing spoken language, how to communicate socially, good habits, shows, songs, music, rhythmic activities using playing and free activities.

2.6.3 The History of Creative Space for Children in Germany

There is no doubt that the German Friedrich Froebel is one of the greatest educators and the founder of preschool education. His ideas are still effective in education and the training sciences and have a special originality. Froebel founded "Children's Garden" in 1837 in Germany. It was renamed

"Kindergarten" in 1840. As one of the founders of the child-centered method, he believed that a child's personality is perfected and expressed in the form of emotions during a process called "play". Froebel argued that the preschool period is a knowledge center where children are educated, develop, and innovate with creativity. He made devices for children to play with, each of which was designed with a specific purpose. According to Froebel, the curriculum of preschool education includes softballs, pottery mud, sand, water play, drama games, social games, and communication with nature.

2.6.4 The History of Creative Space for Children in Iran

Kindergartens in Iran were established for the first time in 1923 in Tabriz by a teacher named Jabbar Asgarzadeh (Baghcheban). Since he was an educated person and familiar with children and children's literature, he started his first activities in this field. He devoted most of his efforts to children during his lifetime and achieved some success in this field. His daughter "Samin" continued his path after his death. The gap between the initial activities and the expansion of activities for children in Iran was as large as in other parts of the world.

Special attention was paid to children in Iran after the establishment of the Children's Book Council in 1962 and the Institute for the Intellectual Development of Children and Young Adults in 1966. This was mainly for the intellectual development of children.

2.7 Different Groups Using Kindergartens

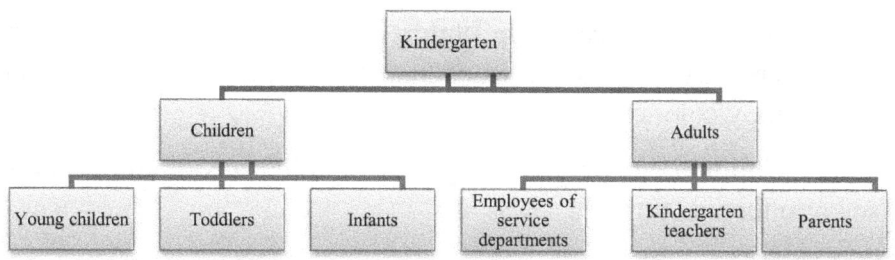

Figure 2-1 Diagram of different groups using kindergartens

As seen in the figure above, the groups using kindergartens are a combination of adults and children. So, the spaces should be designed in such a way that there is no interference between the activities in addition to coordinating the spaces concerning these two groups.

2.8 Children's Activities in Preschool Age - Wants and Needs

Three main activities are carried out in every childcare center as follows:

- Sleeping, eating and playing

- Sleeping and eating

The characteristic of children at first is to sleep only with occasional meals. Children's need for sleep decreases gradually as they grow, feeding frequency is controlled, and playtime is increased until formal education begins.

2.8.1 Educational Activities and Games for Toddlers

- The teacher can use picture books in happy colors and large pictures or puppets to tell stories to children;

- The teacher can help children understand the concepts by using large Legos and wooden or plastic pieces in different and happy colors;

- Children can be given large perforated beads or empty spools to thread them;

- Children at this age enjoy playing with open equipment such as swings and slides;

- Puzzles with a few pieces;

- Games that develop the five senses;

- At this age, painting starts with scrawling.

2.8.2 Educational Activities and Games for Young Children

- Puzzles, wooden cubes, Lego, and picture books;

- Dollhouses, building tools such as screws and hammers, and cars;

- Playdough, crafts, painting, collage;

- Outdoor games such as throwing and catching balls, walking on a balance stick, slides, swings, water play, sand play, and group games with the teacher;

- Storytelling and puppet show.

2.9 Developmental Psychology of Children

2.9.1 Developmental Psychology of Children Under 6 Years Old

The early stages of development affect human life to such an extent that psychologists argue that 70% of a child's personality is formed during this period and that they permanently affect his/her mental processes, i.e., perception, motivations, emotions, conflicts, thinking, feeling, etc. The interaction of heredity and the environment affects human development. Development may be external and visible or internal and invisible. Slowing down the speed of development in one area sometimes causes development in another field.

Human development is affected, speeded up, or slowed down by many factors. The process of human development is affected by various subgroups such as heredity and biological preparation that directly affect physical, emotional, and mental development, as well as environmental factors that affect mental, moral, and social development. The highest speed of human physical development occurs in the first year of birth, emotional development in the second year of life, readiness to accept others and socialization in the third year of life, and examples of complex behaviors and analytical thinking in the fourth year of life.

A person will suffer irreparable damage if his/her physiological needs are not met in the first year of life. The emotional development of the child in the second year of life requires providing security in addition to the love and direct support of parents. Risk factors affect the child's emotional development.

Children's social needs are evident and their love and interest in others can be seen in the third year of life. They demand playing with their peers because of their behavior. This stage directly and significantly affects the entire social life of the child, showing the child's entry into a more advanced stage of development.

At this stage, the personal infrastructure of the child's language reactions is also formed. At the age of 4, the mental and cognitive development of the child accelerates, which brings with it the need for resistance, dignity, and respect.

The child engages in mental interactions and achieves forms with intuitive thinking at this stage.

2.9.2 Social Development of the Child

Social development includes all behaviors of people in front of others as actions and reactions. Children show actions such as crying, laughing, screaming, talking, cooperation, etc. to meet their basic needs. They begin to develop socially with simple behaviors from 3 months of age and communicate with others, including the mother, by reacting to surrounding sounds and smiling. They look at those who talk to them and recognize strangers and acquaintances at the age of 4 months. They follow conditioned behaviors and respond to familiar movements at the age of 6 months. They also try to get attention from others by imitating adults and doing certain things. They react to hearing their name, are very happy to be spoken to by others, and sometimes verbalize their meaning around one year of age.

Furthermore, children enjoy playing with acquaintances and parents, providing simple assistance to adults, know people more fully, use more words, develop a sense of competition, and impose themselves on others by the age of two. They prefer playing with their peers at the age of 3 because of more independence. Self-centeredness is evident in children at this age. They enjoy more stable friendships and can understand the effects of communication with others. So, 3 to 6 years old is a very important period and significantly affects the socialization of the child.

2.9.3 Mental and Cognitive Development of the Child According to Piaget

One of the greatest theorists of child development is the Swiss psychologist, Jean Piaget. He achieved the mental structures and cognitive development of children by observing and studying the child's interactions to understand his/her surroundings and divided the child's mental development into 4 main stages:

1. The sensorimotor stage - 0 to 2 years old

2. The preoperational thinking stage – toddler through age 7

3. The concrete operational stage - ages 7 to 13

4. The formal operational stage - ages 13 and up

Since the discussion is focused on the preschool period, the second stage will be examined briefly.

In the preoperational stage, the child achieves more development, communicates better with the development of language and language skills, and achieves new findings by acquiring the ability to recognize the environment through inner images and denial and manipulation of the environment. At this stage, the child is very interested in observation and acquires the experience and preparation required for writing. The child looks at everything from his/her mental point of view, is self-centered, does not know about the existence of other points of view, or cannot think about them. Thus, he/she does not have a correct understanding of reality and is not open to criticism.

At this stage, children have a one-dimensional vision and gradually prepare to find better ways. They will then realize the numerical concepts and understand the concept of form and context. With the development of visual thinking at the age of 4.5 to 6 years old, they achieve creativity and express their feelings by drawing and playing (Piaget, Jean, 1989).

2.9.4 Child Development Stages in Preschool Period

The different stages of human development in the preschool period are generally as follows:

1. The first 5 weeks of a child's life (newborns);

2. From birth to 2 years old (infancy);

3. From 1.5 to 3 years old (mobility);

4. From 3 to 5 years old (young children)

5. From 5 to 6 years old (preparation)

The child's changes happen gradually with the fading of the previous stage and the bolding of the following stages and are a chain of a natural sequence that overlap each other, with each stage dependent on the previous and subsequent stages.

2.10 Children and Playing

Playing is trying to touch, feel, control, and learn about the world. The child has a special life called playing and always tames up a small life, playing. One of the most important objective and practical motivations for children is the possibility of realizing this particular life, namely playing and exploring the environment.

Playing or recreational activities satisfy the will of the action. Playing entertains one from childhood to adolescence. Old education considered playing to be a waste of time and energy and prevented the child from playing as much as possible. However, the new education recognizes it as one of the necessary factors for the development of the body and mind, believing in the psychological fact that playing is a natural desire with a great educational purpose.

A successful educational environment stimulates and conquers this desire and performs its educational activities as playing and accompanied by it. As a vital process, playing is important for the physical, ideal, emotional, and psychological development of children. So, a separate topic should be dedicated to it.

2.11 The Role of Play in Child Development

Satisfying the basic needs of children significantly contributes to the formation and development of their personalities. Most children's needs are satisfied through playing. Concerning the important role of playing in children's development and the reasons for the need for play spaces, UNESCO notes: "Play spaces satisfy the needs of children's development in all areas."

1. Physical development, 2. cognitive development, 3. social development, and 4. emotional development.

It should be noted that children's playgrounds do not meet their expectations in many cases. Thus, children do not respond positively to receiving and actively using themselves.

2.12 The Importance of Playing

According to the above, the importance and benefits of playing for the cultivation of physical and mental strength, social development, and cultivation of good moral character and temperament are as follows:

1. Playing increases the child's physical strength and makes him/her healthy;

2. Playing satisfies the child's inner desires and amuses and pleases him/her;

3. Playing has an educational value through which educational materials can be taught to the child;

4. Group play socializes the child and strengthens his/her sense of responsibility;

5. Playing significantly contributes to a child's personality and thinking;

6. Playing strengthens characteristics such as courage, respect for justice, a sense of cooperation, respect for the law, stability, and self-control;

7. Playing gives the child freedom of action to show initiative without considering the available tools;

8. Playing prepares the child for real life and connects him/her to the outside world.

2.13 Essential Tips for the Design of Play Equipment

1. Happy and warm colors should be used in the construction of play equipment to attract children's attention;

2. The materials used in the play equipment should not be rough. Their surfaces and edges should be smooth and without any sharpness or edge;

3. They should create a sense of physical and mental security in the child (play equipment that makes constant and ear-splitting sounds makes children nervous and bored);

4. Play equipment should be made in such a way as to have an educational role and helps the child in understanding mathematical and scientific concepts or social regulations;

5. Play equipment must be washable and disinfectable (safety and health);

6. Play equipment should be attractive in terms of shape and appearance and increase children's imagination;

7. Play equipment should be designed in such a way as to create a sense of independence in children.

Play equipment must be installed naturally and sometimes in combination depending on their type of work, so that young people as well as teenagers are entertained in their group environment. Moreover, the necessary precautions should be taken to strengthen and resist game equipment for young children and adolescents.

2.14 Children's Painting

2.14.1 Children and Painting

Have you ever looked at a child's painting and been surprised by the reflection of the young artist's thoughts and feelings? Have you ever wondered what your child is trying to tell you by drawing a house with no windows, a man with no trunk and having two hands sticking out of his head, or a tree with needle leaves? Children's drawings have an immediate appeal and are simple, attractive, and full of life and identity. Through their drawings, children say things that they cannot say for various reasons. Like dreams and dreams, painting enables them to free themselves from inhibitions and talk to us about their problems, discoveries, and fears in an unconscious state. The child soon realizes that drawing is a means of expression that corresponds to his/her thoughts, sets him/her free in his imagination, and provides him/her with abundant pleasure. Besides, the child can show his/her inner thoughts and self through painting. In any case, only adults pay attention to the interpretation and analysis of children's drawings. Children reveal many aspects of their personalities when commenting through pictures. They do not do this to satisfy us or to provide the possibility of psychological recognition and investigation, but they care about pouring out the accumulated experiences that represent their existence...

The first signs drawn on the paper by the child are mostly caused by the pencil hitting the paper. The child soon realizes that there are objects and things around him/her that can leave a certain impression on the surface. Therefore, he/she starts to scrawl with any means he gets with great pleasure. The irregular lines drawn by the child at the age of 16 to 18 months gradually give way to two more specific graphic works, i.e., writing and line drawing. Each of these will find its place over time due to the child's intellectual development and maturity.

Children name the lines and circles they draw at the age of two or three. During this period, they no longer draw lines on paper just to enjoy the movement or pressure of the pencil but want to express their inner feelings about their short-term life experiences. Eventually, children's line drawings become regular and even meaningful to adults at the age of four. At this age, an image of a human and sometimes some letters of the alphabet are visible. In this way, the child completely passes the scrawling stage and enters the allegorical stage. This is exactly the stage where the child draws a few lines as a story under his/her drawings, imitating the adults. These writings are often drawn from left to right and sometimes vice versa.

Children try to respect spacing in their writing. Interestingly, they ask adults to read their writings. In these cases, parents can get a clue by carefully looking at the content of the drawing to create a story and tell it to the child. Children usually listen carefully to these stories and do not protest if something is read against their wishes, knowing that their writings cannot be read. It is enough for them that someone reads their writings and shares their feelings. Children try to draw a picture of a person or persons at the age of three to four. This picture has certain elements such as a circle instead of a head with some lines as arms and legs around it.

The simplicity of children's drawing at this age cannot be attributed to their lack of knowledge of technique. This is the image they have of their body in their mind. The picture drawn by the children has a head, which is important to them because the head is the location of the senses of sight and hearing, thereby enabling communication with the outside world. Furthermore, it has arms that enable grasping and touching objects and also has legs that enable moving. When a child draws a person, he/she expresses his shape or his/her understanding of his/her body and desires first of all. There is a clear connection between some of the lines of the painted person and the physical and mental characteristics of the child who drew it.

If the person drawn is harmonious, the child is likely to be completely harmonious, but when the person is drawn in a very small size or the corner of the paper, the child thinks of himself as low value and cannot establish proper communication with others. If the person is drawn in a large size, we are dealing with an irritable and sensitive child who always thinks that he/she has been oppressed. Weak and introverted children often don't draw any foot for the person or draw it sitting, and aggressive children show the person with dry, angular lines.

Children always draw members of a harmonious family together holding hands. The degree of intimacy between these people is higher if they hold each other's hands, kiss each other, or play together. In family drawing, the child draws him/herself near the person whom he/she feels is more comfortable next to him/her or whom he/she loves the most. However, the child, for example, draws his/her sister between his/her parents and him/herself away from them on the edge of the paper if he/she thinks that his/her sister is more important to his/her parents than him/her. Some family members are drawn inside the house and some outside in some paintings. These drawings either reflect the real absence of the person or persons drawn outside the house or the child's lack of emotional attraction towards them. In most of the children's drawings, there is always a main character on whom they place their most emotional burden, either in the form of love and praise or fear and anxiety. This character is often drawn before others because it is the first person the child thinks of. This main character is always bigger than other people and is drawn with more details and more complete. Consciously or unconsciously, the child wishes for the absence of a person who does not draw it in the family painting.

This can be seen mostly in the drawings of children who have not yet accepted the birth of their younger sibling after several years. So, they draw themselves in the golden age in which they lived before the birth of the baby by removing this annoying child from their drawing (Thomas, Glyn v, Silk, Angele M.j., 1991).

2.15 Child and Space

2.15.1 Child and Architecture

One of the main functions of any architectural space is to meet the users' needs and interests in a suitable manner. To this end, the associated users as well as their needs and preferences should be identified. Understanding this information about adults and the spaces they need is not a difficult task because they all (apart from environmental, cultural and educational differences) have almost similar perceptions about architectural spaces, while this is not the case with children, as their mental structure and the way they reason and feel are fundamentally different from adults. Thus, architects are required to become familiar with these differences when working for children and pay special attention to them.

2.15.1.1 How to Design a Suitable Space for children

We as adults do not have the sweet feelings and moods of our childhood any more. However, we are able to recognize and understand these thoughts and ideas, turn them into practical and visible forms, and create a space that is a real example of children's dreams and thoughts. Such a space can arouse their enthusiasm and, as a result, develop their creativity. In order to create the desired space for children, we should try to think like them and observe their behavior in playing games, in making different shapes, as well as in playing building games such as boxes, chairs, and the tools they have. Their ideas for making windows, walls, corners, recesses, and protrusions and landscaping can be good models for us. Understanding children's behavior and reactions is regarded as one of the major sources of inspiration for children's architecture. Their desires, the factors that upset them, the factors that arouse their enthusiasm and taste, their love and relationship with life, their reactions and thoughts can be good sources of inspiration for designing the suitable architecture for them. Before anything else, a child needs emotional satisfaction and a sense of connection with his/her physical and social environment in order to develop. Therefore, a suitable environment for children is characterized by the presence of the necessary stimuli and incentives that are compatible with each stage of their development.

When designing architecture, the most useful trick in order to develop an emotional bond between the child and the environment and to make him/her satisfied is to consider his/her physical and emotional dependencies and tendencies at each stage of his/her development. Paying enough attention to the geography of space when designing architecture and creating diversity in the visual and emotional characteristics of its different corners can have a great impact on children's adaptation to the space, resulting in an increase in the child's sense of attachment.

Another important factor that can be affective to keeping children's connection with the environment and developing a sense of psychological security in them is the clarity and readability of the environment for them, i.e., an environment that they can easily understand and interpret. Accordingly, one of the characteristics of a suitable environment is its adaptation to children's cognitive and perceptual capabilities, while expanding their mental plans and recognition and homogenizing the emergence of creativity in them.

2.15.1.2 Characteristics of a Suitable Space for Children

With design and materials, we must create a space with the following characteristics:

1. Making children feel safe in it.
2. Having harmony with nature.
3. Classification of the rooms, classrooms and spaces, so that children's ability to identify and orient increases, and at the same time, they feel like a member of a large group.
4. Designing the interior spaces in such a way that children's curiosity is aroused. Structural elements such as columns, beams, girders, and walls should represent the task they perform, so that children can feel the energy and power of these elements and understand the structure skeleton, load-bearing elements, and structural components with their sense of curiosity.
5. Developing a joyful and hopeful atmosphere with design and materials, so that children feel in a safe and soulful space.
   The transparency and processing of natural light in spaces and the use of color elements are among the suitable tools for colored of soulful and hopeful spaces. Colors evoke different concepts for children, e.g., blue: sky, green: grass and forest, yellow: sun, and white: clouds.

The building inside should be bright and open. Dark spaces, narrow indentations and protrusions in the wall, and ambushes and hidden places in the building should be avoided. The difference in levels in foyers, halls, exhibitions and the difference in levels in twin rooms, light radiation from above, creating dark and bright spaces with strips of direct light, slanted glass panels, and different levels like studios, open and wide spaces inside the building are among desirable characteristics for architectures that are suitable for children.

In contrast to narrow and cave-like spaces, high platforms are among dead and soulless spaces and make children tired and bored. Non-Euclidean spaces cause intellectual stimulation and the disappearance of ambiguity, which has misleading effects.

2.15.2 Sensual and Intellectual Perception of Architectural Space

Understanding space is a very difficult task. The child has to discern himself from the world around him and at the same time analyze this world. He/she does this action by recognizing the objects around him/herself, and to succeed in this experience, he/she needs to employ all his/her feelings and intelligence. The child should feel comfortable, fearless and calm in dealing with the objects and buildings, as well as in communication and life inside them. Darkness along with disproportionate forms scares him/her more than anything else. Spaces with happy and bright (and not harsh) colors and sometimes colors with unclear forms (such as the state appearing in watercolor painting) inspires dreamy and imaginative themes and emotional, friendly, kind, and dreamy feelings in the child, so that he/she feels like being a flyer. Meanwhile, in architecture for older children, soft colors with clear borders, more details in the building, and soft curves in designing the space can be used. Colors with higher density, thinner and more delicate lines, and attention to detail in design are characteristic of architectures that are suitable for teenagers.

The main point is that the designed space and building should have color, line, shape, and spatial relationship with the spirit of children and teenagers. The colors used in the building should give a special warmth to the space, as a set of colors makes a space warm or cold. An architect should not think in a thick manner, as in this way, a thick and hard architecture with harder understanding and colors with higher density would emanate from his/her thick mind. Architecture for 1-3year old children should be easy, simple, and without miniature textures details. The fields of view should be clear and natural, so that the child understands the state of the space very quickly. The whole space should be balanced, with reasonable and logical sizes. Spaces and buildings designed in relation to each other should not carry contradictions and emotional conflicts. Intensive color contrasts should be avoided. The perspective of space should be simple and perceivable. The confusing, sharp, and illusory lighting should be avoided.

Architecture for 4-6 year- old children should be realistic, imaginative, and romantic (we mean sweet dreams, not illusions) at the same time. A little contradiction can be used with caution and with awareness and mastery of educational issues. The design of the forms and spaces should be simple, but not as simple as for the previous age range. Meanwhile, the space designs for this age range should have no vulgarity and space freezing, but they should have life, freshness, and polish. The spaces should be designed by using a special method, a special style, and special materials. The mass and similar designs make children stupid and obedient and without thinking. Mild, loose, slippery, cheerful, light and soft colors, and not dense, thick and hard colors should be used when designing architecture for these children.

A child finds a place in space for anything and anyone that interests him/her and is happy to find them in their own place; for example, in the hide-and-seek game, the game for them does not mean looking for someone who has hidden him/herself in an unknown place, but it is to find someone whose place is known for him/her. After a lot of research, Guilford concluded that human intellectual abilities cannot be summed up in one dimension and is called intelligence. In his opinion, some intellectual characteristics of humans are directly effective in the emergence of creativity. Fluency of thought flow and flexibility of intellectual powers are among these characteristics that form divergent thinking. Divergent thinking means moving away from a common point, i.e., the custom and tradition of society, while convergent thinking means approaching that point. Divergent thinking is called creativity only when it gives rise to a positive and fruitful result. Guilford believes that creativity represents a divergent talent, providing new and unique solutions, but in this way, convergent thinking is also effective and we should not neglect promoting convergent thinking. The development of divergent thinking leads to the developing convergent thinking. Many successful people in society have good intelligence, but they have not benefited from divergent thinking and creativity. But creative people have good intelligence, if they are not smart. Some researchers believe that a certain level of intelligence is necessary for the emergence of creativity, but beyond that level, i.e., the threshold of creativity, the development and emergence of creativity depend on factors other than intelligence, the most important of which include: development of the child's personality, the environmental and social conditions, and the space where he/she is raised.

2.15.3 Child and Forms

Children like to find a familiar feature in anything. Specially, small children try to make an emotional relationship with the environment like their own home. These familiar forms help children to consider a new and strange environment as a second home from the outside. Thus, in designing architecture for these children, simple and elementary forms are preferred to complex and irregular forms. Changing the height of the ceiling, views, corridors, patios, using special features for important points, and giving a difference to a particular space makes every child assume that a corner of the space is desirable in the first place based on his/her perception of the space, and then gain a good understanding of the direction and routes.

2.15.4 Child and Natural Elements

Natural elements are regarded as the continuous source and stimulus of children's imaginations. If children do not have enough experience in terms of communication with them, these elements will not develop their imaginations. Children show great sensitivity and desire towards nature: sun, fire and animals. They are strongly influenced by their natural experiences and are willing to discover the laws of nature and play with natural elements. Creating living spaces in nature can help them to establish this relationship.

2.15.5 Symbols and Signs

Elements of a building that affect children's imagination and understanding, e.g., special details, decorations, etc., represent symbols of children's understanding and recognition. A child at any age tends to these objects with pride and joy. The signs placed along the way can make his/her feelings awaken and are better recorded in his/her mind, so that he/she would have a better memory of the space.

Children tend to have a variable space, so that they can leave their footprints on it and thus create their own special signs. Diversity in visual points, sound, light, height, etc. can make the environment freer and more vivid for children.

2.15.6 Child and Feelings

Like adults, children are also mature human beings, and like all human beings, they have different emotions on different days and even at different hours of the day. Sometimes they prefer their solitude, while sometimes they need to talk and socialize. A well-designed environment is characterized by having designed both public and private places for people. The more we get involved in designing environments for children, the more we realize that a good environment for adults can be a good environment for children as well.

2.15.7 Light and Color

Cultivation of the concept of shape and color begins very early in childhood. When they are less than 3-years old, children can separate objects according to their shapes, while 3-6 year-old children's attention is more focused on colors.

This issue of color will be the basis for separating the shapes. From children's point of view, bright colors look big and dark colors look lifeless. Therefore, when the issue of color comes up, children prefer mixed colors. Black and white colors look boring everywhere. The child wants diversity and gets tired of spaces of one shape, one color and uniformity. Therefore, contrasting lightings (artificial and natural) that cause tension and fatigue should be avoided when designing architectures for children.

An acceptable way to design the architecture of kindergartens is to use colors and modern teaching methods. The interior design of kindergartens should be designed according to children's mental, behavioral, and psychological characteristics and consider the appropriate colors for them. In this way, we can provide a suitable place for children's development. Colors can play an effective role in increasing children's intelligence, concentration, and calmness with the power of influencing their mood and subconscious mind.

Desirable spaces for children should be bright and light well, as spaced with a lot of sunlight, natural light and transparency can have a positive impact on children's feelings. From their point of view, these spaces are intimate and joyful. On the other hand, dark rooms with low and artificial light seem unfavorable. In indoor spaces that are illuminated with artificial light or halls, it is possible to use a variety of colors in the light.

2.15.8 Dimensions and Sizes

Children naturally like to find things that are especially made for their dimensions and sizes. For example, a door through which adults can pass only if they squat down can open to a playhouse and has two advantages: first, adults rarely enter this space; and secondly, if they do enter it, have to compress their size to become smaller and play at the same height level as children do.

2.15.9 Child and Sounds

When children enter a large space like a church, the first thing they do is step firmly on the hard surface of the floor in order to hear the echo of their feet. We have found that children listen to space again and again, so spaces for children should not be acoustically dead.

If the sound reflection is too much for them, they would automatically produce less sound. Using hard surfaces to create dispersion in sound reflection can make the space a much more acoustically favorable environment for your child compared to a space that is dead with the use of acoustic materials.

2.16 Child's Perception and attention to Space

Certain images presented in training or fiction books, etc., mostly induce the living environment of years ago: the living environment belonging to the time of our grandparents, gabled houses with gardens, streams running through the yards, and yards with ponds and fountains and some domestic animals. Children, most of whom live in complexes, draw houses in the same way, because the authors of the books have depicted their childhood pictures. These images are imposed on the children, and adults convey to the children their lack of connection to the current environment and perhaps the wish that they and their children still live in such a peaceful environment. Sometimes the economic problems that are passed on to children by parents play a significant role in preventing their imagination, so that children imagine a house and a space that is not too expensive.

The architect should, on the one hand, understand the child, the space, and his/her wishes, as well as his/her needs and problems, and find ways to solve them, and on the other hand, become familiar with the environment where the child lives today and understand it. To this end, architects need to increase their speed so that they can reach the feet of educationalists, sociologists, doctors, and psychologists who have more or less fully understood the childhood world.

In general, children's understanding of urban space is very slow, and they have a fragmented image of it for a long time. In fact, they pay more attention to small details than to the whole complex. On the other hand, they convey the reality of the city and sometimes their paintings speak of their ideal environment. This is why most children often depict traffic lights, streets, and television antennas in their drawings instead of ponds and trees. It is very difficult to understand whether children are sensitive to the height of buildings or not. But most of them have an image of a house: a mansion with a loft or a green villa and sometimes an apartment. In fact, the building that the child knows is the one that he/she reads in books or lives in. Children show a great connection to new and clean buildings with light and soft materials and colors.

2.17 Conclusion

The aim of this study is to evaluate diversity-based design ideas for kindergartens and educational support spaces for 3-6 year-old Iranian children with the approach of improving their creativity, so that, by applying the resulting ideas in the design of special spaces for children, children's motivation to play as well as their imagination, curiosity, and creativity will increase. In addition to examining some effective factors in the development of children's creativity, this study presents a report on the research method, preparation of research tools, and its implementation, and then describes the research model, and finally provides some ideas for designing special spaces for children based on the research model.

Research literature shows that children's curiosity, play and imagination are among the factors that are effective in improving their creativity. According to research, children's creativity depends on their imagination, and the best age for development of children's creativity and imagination is in the range between 2-10.

Research on the relationship between play and joking and inspiration of creativity in preschool children shows that inspiration for creativity in children is directly correlated with the extent of their play, as mobility in preschool age is considered as the first mode of activity, expression, learning and progress. Research shows that a person's curiosity plays an effective role in the creativity process, and creative people are usually curious.

Chapter 3.
Data Analysis

3.1 Reviewing Available Samples

3.1.1 Domestic Samples of Iran

- **Ordibehesht Kids House**

This complex is located in Shahrak-e Gharb, in Tehran., obtaining the license from the Cultural and Artistic Organization of Tehran Municipal. This Kids House has started its activity since May 2011, with the aim of carrying out educational and recreational activities for children in the age group of 1-6 in two parts of kindergarten (part-time) and mother and child workshops (creativity and growth, play and music, swimming, story-telling, etc.) and taking advantage of it in order to develop and foster children's creativity and create strong mother-child relationships, as well as to prepare children to enter official social arenas.

Figure 3.1. Outdoor views of the kindergarten

The central building consists of 3 floors: the first is dedicated to children aged between 2-4, the second to children aged between 4-6, and the third one to creativity classes.

The 1st and 2nd floors each have 3 classrooms and a closed playground. Each class is dedicated to painting, crafting, pottery, and poetry performance, according to the schedule. In addition, wayfinding in this center has been facilitated by partitioning and separation of spaces.

The use of different and happy colors, the use of wide windows to let in natural light, and the creation of a suitable scale and space function for increasing interactions among children are among the features affecting creativity that can be seen in this center.

Creativity workshop

Strengthening the enthusiasm for learning, cognitive and social skills, promoting creative thinking, and increasing self-confidence in children are among the most important goals of this workshop.

Creativity and growth workshops mainly include the following activities:

- Guided plays include individual and group plays, together with educational toys suitable for children's age.
- Making children familiar with the rhythm of singing and sound in a happy environment with child music.
- Activities to develop eye movement, visual focus, hand-eye coordination, and harmonization of the left and right hemispheres of the brain.
- Sensory experiences to develop the sense of touch and strengthen the children's hand skills.

- Making crafts and painting.
- Reading poems and stories.

The complex is equipped with CCTV, a kitchen to cook hot food with daily ingredients, a 100-inch children's cinema to show cartoons and educational programs, an air conditioning system, tatami flooring for the playroom, a colorology, sand pools, a ball pool, a site for domestic animals, and various game and sports equipment for children.

Figure 3.2. Sand pools

Figure 3.3. Ball Pool

Figure 3.4. Colorology

Figure 3.5. Water and foam playing

- **Zehne Roshan Kindergarten**

This complex is located in the Sadeghiyeh area of Tehran. The existing building was not designed for children from the beginning and has been changed to a kindergarten for children aged between 2-6 years old. The existence of a closed play area in the center has led to crowding and stimulation, resulting in the increased possibility of renovating the space. Also, the use of wide windows and a central patio for letting in the natural light, the use of happy colors in furniture and curtains, creating the right scale by using the right furniture and the way they are arranged are among the features that affect children's creativity. Also, due to the placement of different classes around a main and central space, the presence of crowding at the turning point of the building (closed play space), and the lack of use of signs for way finding, it is not possible to find proper orientation in the kindergarten spaces, which in turn stimulates children to explore the space and move in it, and hence children' imagination, curiosity, and creativity are flourished.

This complex includes:

- Training life skills by playing (they do plays and activities with children in order to train life skills. Patience, anger control, turn taking, respect were examples of the values that were targeted in today's play....).
- Spray painting and artwork (an interesting game to stimulate children' excitement for preparing a beautiful art work).
- Playing with water and foam (a fun and psychological game).
- Playing with puzzles are useful for strengthening children's brain and cognitive development and their various skills, including physical skills, hand-eye coordination. When the child moves, picks up and rotates the puzzle pieces, he/she learns the hand-eye

connection. His/her eyes see the puzzle and his/her brain imagines what the puzzle should look like or which piece should be found and placed. Then his/her brain, eyes, and hands work together to find that piece and place it in its proper place. Playing with puzzles helps the child to develop his/her fine motor skills, just as it helps hand-eye coordination.

- **Gardening (children's familiarity with flowers and plants).**

Figure 3.6. Paint spraying

Figure 3.7. Training life skills

Figure 3.8. Gardening (planting flowers and plants)

Figure 3.9. Playing with water and foam

- **Ghesseye Man Kindergarten**

This complex started its activities officially in 2013 in the Zaferanyeh district of Tehran. The kindergarten is located in the vicinity of the residential context.

Figure 3.10. Using color and shapes in the facade

Kindergarten Architecture

The kindergarten building was a 2-story residential house that had been converted into a kindergarten. The area of the building is 1500 square meters. The kindergarten entrance has a path to the ground floor and a path to the lower floor.

Figure 3.11. Using colorful tree-like shapes on the wall, which has diversified the space

The kindergarten has 9 classrooms, restrooms with equipment suitable for children (according to their sizes), a special cleaning room for children (changing room for toddlers), a dining hall with children-sized equipment, courtyard with natural grass, playground, child's farming space, creativity workshop, children's sand playground, kitchen, and movie screening room, ground floor, the main spaces of the kindergarten, which includes classrooms, reception area, office, kitchen, dining hall, bathroom, and balcony, which is a semi-open play area.

Chapter 3. Data Analysis ➢ 89

Figure 3.12. Children's playground

In the lobby of the kindergarten, various colors are used for the reception desk and the walls, and the decoration is suitable for children (according to their size).

Figure 3.13 Various colors and artificial light in the kindergarten lobby

The kindergarten has 8 classes for the age group of 3-6 years old. Each class is named after a fruit. The dimensions of the classes are about 25 square meters. Orange, yellow, blue, green, cream and pink colors have been used in the coloring of the classes. The classrooms have natural and artificial lighting.

Classroom furniture

The classroom furniture consists of tables and chairs suitable for children (according to their size) and made of wood. The shape of the tables is curved and their arrangement is flexible, so that children can arrange the tables according to their own taste and educational use, which plays an effective role in strengthening children's creativity.

Other classroom furniture includes wooden shelves for children's items, a place to hang clothes, and boards. The classroom walls are covered with children's paintings and crafts.

Figure 3.14. Color scheme and classroom furniture.

The basement floor contains a room for children aged 2-3, a bedroom, and W.C.

Figure 3.15. Kindergarten yard has green space, a gazebo, sandground, as well as a swimming pool which is under construction

The gazebo is placed on the sandy ground. Through the play equipment, children get to know the concepts of weight, mass, size, and materials.

Figure 3.16. Kindergarten playground

Wooden playset, swings and slides are placed on the lawn.

The classification of children's age groups is as follows:

· Age group 2-3 years old.

· Age group 3-4 years old.

· Age group 4-5 years old.

· Age group 5-6 years old (preschool).

Children's daily hours are scheduled according to their age group: morning workouts (morning exercises), Persian, English, and French training programs, snacks, lunch, outdoor plays, use of the playground, reading stories, making crafts, playing with training materials, and watching training videos.

In addition to the daily training programs, special training programs under the title of extracurricular classes are also held for children, e.g., music, painting, agriculture and creativity workshops. Children are trained about plants and planting plants in the green space of the kindergarten.

Aerobics and yoga are performed downstairs in the salon with foam flooring. And a four-season pool is under construction in the courtyard as well.

Kindergarten educational scheduling is done based on play and creative education.

Figure 3.17. Children's creativity develops through space-making with wood, flowers and shells

In addition to the communication function, kindergarten corridors have a diverse space for children's education.

Figure 3.18. Wall Play Equipments

3.1.2 Foreign Samples

- **Barbapapà Kindergarten (Vignola, Modena, Italy)**

Barbapapà Kindergarten Project was designed in line with the holding of a competition in 2006 under the supervision of Vignola Municipality. A space for about 60 children is considered in the physical plan of this project. The location of this project is specified on a hill above the city. However, its location is not so far away from the welfare-treatment centers of the downtown. In this project, paying attention to the senses and being fully aware of the sustainability factors has been taken into account. This value is intangibly visible around the project and is regarded as a suitable starting point for children's communication with sustainable values.

Figure 3.19. The training and play interior space of Barbapapà Kindergarten

Chapter 3. Data Analysis ➢ 95

Figure 3.20. Color and light in the interior space

The decreased effects of sound by using a grass layer emerging from the ground in this project is one of the points that has provided a favorable environment for children in terms of sensory communication. At the same time, this grass layer has reduced the noise pollution at the entrance of the hill from the lower street of the area. In addition to the functional impact, this space will play an important role in using some of the children's senses in communication with the environment, including their senses of touch and hearing. Stimulating the child's different senses in the environment is one of the exercises that can increase the quality of correct environmental perception in children in the future.

Placement of Buildings and Vegetation

Since one of the sensory stimulation factors in children is the variety of colors, the designers of this project, considering this important point in the design of this kindergarten, tried to strengthen this sense in children by using colored glass used in the main facade overlooking the classrooms. The way the colors are used next to each other is in such a way that they are recognizable and at the same time uplifting and stimulating.

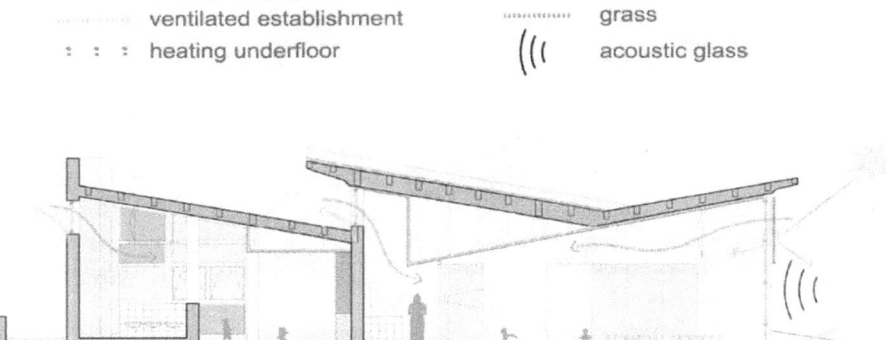

Figure 3.21. Climatic design of the building

Figure 3.22. Colored glass used in the building

The use of colors and materials of the same color as nature, such as wood in the walls, floor and ceiling in the building, encourages children to interact with the environment. Since color plays an effective role in stimulating children's nerves, special attention should be paid to selecting colors for use in different spaces. For example, the blue color and its families is a relaxing color for a child's bedroom, while warm colors such as red and orange are desired for places where children play or for dining areas. In addition, paying attention to colors such as green and brown makes the child compatible with the natural environment. In this project, in addition to paying attention to the sensory stimulation factors, special attention has been paid to the factors affecting environmental sustainability.

- Internal comfort control: In this project, the green covering of the building ensures suitable thermal insulation in order to protect the internal heat, and in order to maintain the comfort of the environment, built-in packages are used on wooden roofs.
- Receiving energy from the environment: Natural energy sources are used during the day. Suitable opening windows are used all along the facade in order to buffer sunlight at different times of the day and keep the interior space warm. In this kindergarten, photovoltaic systems are used on the metal roof in order to supply energy to the indoor spaces. In addition, rainwater collection systems are used to supply water to the bathrooms. At the same time, the use of colors and materials designed with special shapes has been studied and made in line with a sustainable system.

98 ◁ Designing Children's Creative Space

Figure 3.23. Design of roof and lighting of the building

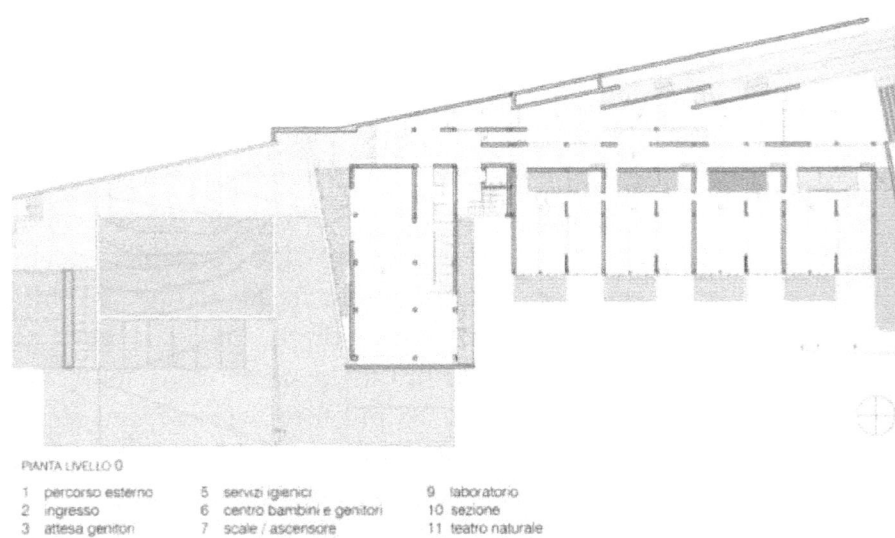

Figure 3.24. The building plan

- **Kindergarten 8Units (Velez-Rubio, Almería, Spain)**

This kindergarten is located in the village of Bless-Rubio in Almeria province, Spain. One of the goals of this project has been to help develop children's mental, social, and mental abilities. Children often define a house first by its steep roof and then by its doors and windows. A kindergarten is like a big house where children spend most of their time and its space can also reflect their imaginations.

Figure 3.25. Exterior facade of the kindergarten 8units

In this complex, there are eight classes assigned to three groups of children and classified according to their age groups. A dining area, a kitchen and several administrative spaces are located around a central courtyard where children play and spend part of their leisure time. All the classes have access to the open space, bringing about a kind of connection between the interior and the exterior.

It was decided that the shapes of the facades and windows should be different from what is normal and what children are usually familiar with. Therefore, circular-shaped windows with special frames and strips in green, yellow, and blue colors have been used in the building. During the day, the indoor spaces are colorful for children, and at night, the colorful spaces of the kindergarten bring about a special scene for the neighborhood and the residents of nearby houses. The colors of the different classes have been selected based on children's age.

Children's visual world is different from adults', so some colors and patterns have been designed and adjusted up to a height of 130 cm. Well-washable materials have been used for the facades.

Figure 3.26. Exterior facade and children's play space

The under floor heating system is used to warm the kindergarten space when necessary, which is the best approach for warming such spaces. Using the movement of hot water in this system makes it possible to enjoy the heat caused by the radiant energy of the sun through the panels installed on the roof. Blue color is used for special classes for children under one-year old, which is beneficial for relaxation and induces the color of the sea and the world of dreams. Classes for 1-2 year-old children are painted orange, which plays a useful role in stimulating mobility and activity. For children aged between 2-3 years old, a green color is used, which reminds them of connections with nature. A combination of colors has been used in public spaces such as corridors, dining rooms, etc., which reminds of the diversity in society. Concrete materials, metal and aluminum coils and frames, as well as bricks and some traditional methods have been used so that holes can be easily created in the walls.

Figure 3.27. Dining hall – interior space

The ground is almost square in shape, with two distorted sides and two straight sides almost perpendicular to each other. An interesting idea is used in the design. On the one hand, a central courtyard is placed in the middle of the space, which is a place for children to play and spend their free time in the outdoors, and due to the large windows around it, it is possible to get good light for the corridors and the adjacent spaces, such as the dining room. On the other hand, the presence of the courtyard has made it possible for the manager and supervisors of the kindergarten to monitor the children while they are playing. Access to the courtyard is possible from three corners, and in the fourth corner, there is a toilet that can be used both from inside the corridor and from the court yard, making its use easy at different times. The ground distortion on two fronts and a side space on the third front are used in such a way that three limited open spaces are created in the form of three backyards, and each of the eight classrooms has one door facing this open space, while providing direct light to the classrooms from these spaces. Necessary service spaces have been designed and built next to the classrooms.

Figure 3.28. Plan and positioning of kindergarten 8units

The use of innovative forms for the aperture and windows another important feature of the kindergarten. The abundant use of circular surfaces for this end has caused this kindergarten to have an interesting and original shape for children. Another important feature of the building is the application of different colors, which makes the interior spaces and surfaces as well as some exterior spaces attractive.

Figure 3.29. Use of colors in the interior space - children's play space and part of the facade of the kindergarten

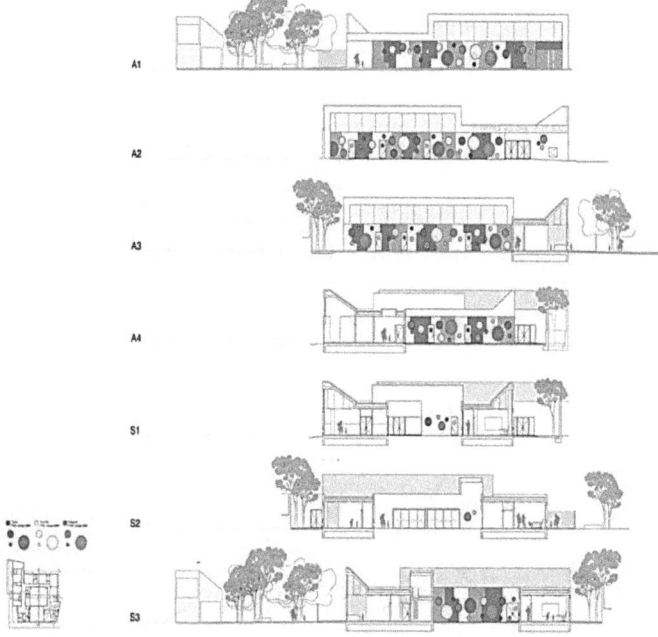

Figure 3.30. Some facades and sections of kindergarten 8units

- **CEBRA Kindergarten (Vonsild, Kolding, Denmark)**

The designers of this kindergarten consider the preconceived idea of "what a school should look like" in its design as a way to stimulate children's curiosity and creativity. The kindergarten building is built on different themes focusing on different activities such as art, design, and architecture. This approach is partly new to the way Danish kindergartens are built, so that the building is more an educational facility, where new information is acquired not through a formal teaching but through play. In addition to the architectural strategy, the definition of a kindergarten also mentions the relationship between the client and the architect. Parents actively participate in the design process by providing ideas and criticism in order to advance the project.

Figure 3.31. CEBRA kindergarten design ideas

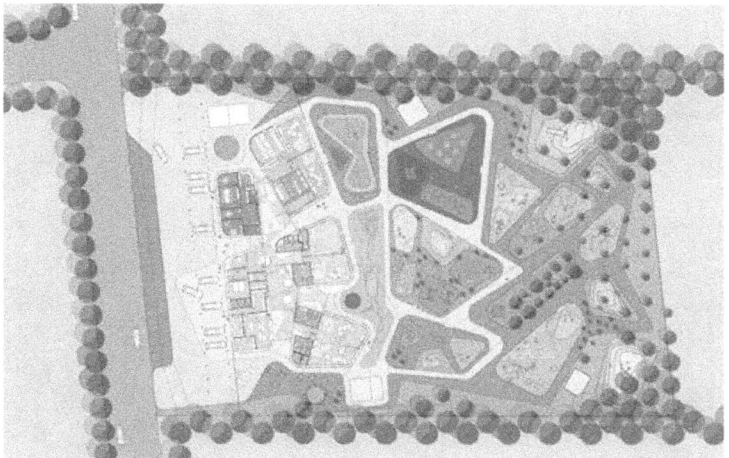

Figure 3.32. CEBRA kindergarten site plan

The irregular shape of the building with an area of 1200 m² is the result of the application of this architectural philosophy in training: "The application of the building should be educational, as we often avoid using the characteristics of ordinary buildings". From their early stages, kids should learn that a house should not be like a kid's drawing of a house with a gable roof and a door in the middle with windows on the both sides. This building has a jagged roof with no corners, because all the angles and corners are rounded. Its main volumes have very few angles.

Figure 3.33. Exterior facade

There are five drop-shaped elements, two of which contain staff equipment, and the remaining three are real spaces for kids. The drops for children are placed in the corners of the garden, with a scattered distribution on the site in order to they a view to the lot. In the garden, the drops are repeated as two-dimensional reflections of the building shapes, so the volumes seem to be gradually faded in the open space. The drops each serve a specific educational purpose, teaching children colors, shapes, and geometry through play.

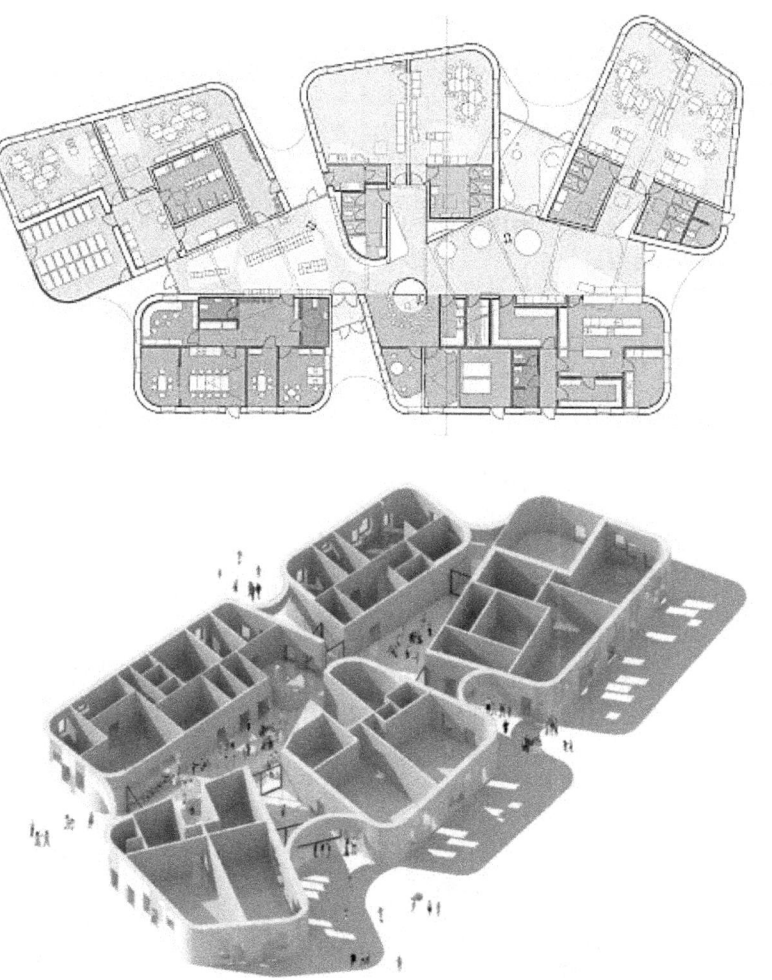

Figure 3.34. Kindergarten plan

The building is divided horizontally into two parts. A pedestal stands on the ground, which is made of five bubbles with roofs connected together so that a special "roof view" is created. The entire pedestal is white and the curved walls look like a paper tube. It also serves as a surface for kids to decorate with their drawings and sculptures. The colorful and sharp corner skyline has been drawn by graphic artist Husk MitNavn. The skyline serves as a source of inspiration as well as an important reminder for children and adults that "art can be great and serious at any time".

- **Kierling Kindergarten (Kierling, Klosterneuburg, Austria)**

Kierling Kindergarten is located in the residential area of Klosterneuburg with its surrounding landscape influenced by its built environment. One of the main characteristics of this kindergarten building is the positioning of the main facade on the south front and in front of the central courtyard. It seems that the plan of merging the boundaries between interior and exteriors spaces is to create a unified and harmonious space for children to be in constant contact with each other. The organization of the space of this kindergarten supports the educational model that encourages children to explore, have independence, and have social interaction.

Figure 3.35. Exterior facade of Kierling Kindergarten

Figure 3.36. Use of glass and transparent materials and creating a break facade with the aim of increasing visual visibility to the natural environment

Six classrooms and two recreation rooms are located along the south facade, which is surrounded by a terrace and work space inside the building. The main entrance, corridors and office space are located on the north side of the building, each of which lies in a linear pattern with a structure contrasting with the southern exposure space. The lights that illuminate the corridors and the passage space induce the sense of greater connection with nature and the environment. The use of broken lines in the organization of the main facade and the application of transparent materials such as glass in order to take advantage of the natural daylight and have the outdoor view inside the group rooms brings about vitality for children.

Figure 3.37. Use of maximum light for a group room

Also, having a cone of vision from different directions due to the rooms around the central courtyard makes it possible for children to do balanced physical movements with each other. The design tries to make children feel safe, connected, and free. Being away from the street and having a view of the garden and the open space helps children to understand nature, weather, and changing seasons. There are special rules for entering the dressing room and sub-areas. Group rooms are available for play, where children can use different things. Through the broken form, the visual views created on the cone of vision of the group rooms are covered even in bad weather. They are also protected against high heat and excessive sunlight. The different sports spaces are planned in two parts: the play space for movement in the garden space, and the open amphitheater for movement in the indoor and closed space, above the entrance level of the building. The kindergarten structure is concrete, which is made with prefabricated and modern connections using the state-of-the-art methods. The kindergarten decoration and the application of shiny materials with bright, warm and lively colors have contributed to the dynamism and vitality of its environment, with the aim of stimulating children's sense of curiosity by creating linear spaces. One of the important characteristics of the kindergarten is the stimulation of a sense of movement and environmental dynamics inside the group rooms, the connection of the interior spaces with the surrounding natural space, and the application of natural daylight with a favorable climate approach.

Figure 3.38. Linear organization of kindergarten space

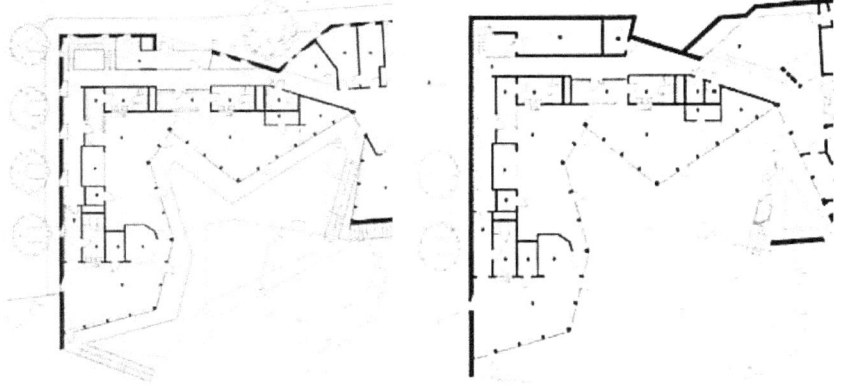

Figure 3.39. Ground and first floor plan of the Kierling kindergarten

- **Trenten Kindergarten (Val Pusteria, South Tyrol, Italy)**

This new kindergarten was built in the hill village of Val Pusteria in South Tyrol in Italy. At first glance, this kindergarten seems to have come out of the earth; on the one hand, the building is clean and on the other hand, it has a good view. This place gives children a good view of the scenery around the village and fosters a deep sensory relationship in terms of environmental perception in childhood, which in turn can provide a proper coordination of internal and external spaces in the design.

Figure 3.40. Trenten Kindergarten exterior facade

While considering the site capability to communicate with children, in this project, the designer teaches them what factors to consider and what architectural elements to engage with in order to better understand their surroundings. As a unique and special building, this childcare center provides a peaceful environment by preparing the surrounding space. The use of the urban landscape is the design concept of this complex, which is defined by the concept and cultural identity originated from the space. This complex is located in an area containing public (educational-sports) facilities.

The positioning of the building is such that the slope of the land towards the east of the kindergarten is aligned with the ground floor of the building. While only half of the building is visible to passers-by. The public space is designed between the school and the kindergarten. The eastern side of the kindergarten is open to this space for retreats and office uses. The entrance to the kindergarten is made from the level parallel to the sidewalk. All the classrooms are located on the south direction, while the multi-purpose spaces have a north-east orientation towards the sidewalk area and a west direction on the ground floor.

Figure 3.41. Positioning of the building

Different construction units (houses) have been designed in such a way that they are near the primary kindergarten and can connect with it from certain distances. In fact, children's sense and identity have been taken into account in this design. The different forms of houses help children to test their perception capability in identifying and understanding certain spaces. In fact, children in each of these houses have the feeling that they are at home.

Public facilities created for the entrance level on the ground floor include two classrooms, sanitary facilities, and dressing rooms. The staff space with two offices and a multi-purpose space and a waiting place for parents is located in the space at the entrance between the two houses. The dressing room, which benefits from daylight, is connected to the daily activity space and serves as a small passageway between the two houses. The stair box and the elevator connect the basement and the entrance floor. This floor contains the sports and relaxation spaces along with a multi-purpose room, a kitchen and a classroom in the south direction. There is an overhang on the slope side only on the west and south sides of the basement, and the skylight brings daylight into the dressing room and classrooms. The classes and rooms are reliably designed for children's activities. The classrooms on the ground floor are located on two levels and are connected to the galleries and open space by through the bridges. The galleries are placed on an exposed concrete structure like a bird nest, and two bridges connect the physical activity space. Development of a sense of displacement in the child and introducing pauses and movement in spaces are among the advantages of this project.

Figure 3.42. Integration of interior and exterior spaces through the interstitial space

There are different views from the windows of the kindergarten towards the foothills, which play an effective role in improving children's visual understanding of the surrounding environment by using their eyesight sense. The classroom that has been located on the basement is bigger than the other classrooms, and the rest of the classrooms open to the gardens on the both sides, so that children have full access to the surrounding garden and wooden patios next to their classrooms. In this type of design considered a deep sensory relationship with the surrounding environment in terms of stimulating children's sense of competence in interacting with the environment, which in addition to vitality, increases children's ability in recognizing objects. In the meantime, blind and visually impaired children can interact better with the surrounding environment.

Figure 3.43. Roof window used in the space between houses

The design of open spaces in this kindergarten is considered as a multi-facet creativity, as the designer has integrated the landscape around the interior and exterior spaces by creating a cross path between the buildings and has converted the roof into a garden-like green space for the upper floor. In addition to integrating the man-made environment with the nature and

116 ◁ Designing Children's Creative Space

harmonizing with the climate, this way of design inspires a passive movement in children to reach different places on the site. The design of children's play spaces in this project has been done according to the relationship between children's perception by his senses and the surrounding materials. In the design of such spaces, in addition to paying attention to the safety of games and educational spaces, the application children's sense of touch and vision in identifying the play equipment, as well as development of a close relationship with the materials and increasing children's ability to recognize are taken into account. In some cases, designers consider the stimulation of children's sense of smell in the environment, which can in turn strengthen their abilities in this sensory area. In this project, the materials are selected based on inspiration from the environment. The traditional elements taken from the surrounding landscapes have resulted in the development of new qualities. In fact, the building originates from personality patterns and is combined with the phenomenon of today's modernity.

Figure 3.44. Children's play space in Trenten Kindergarten

All the exterior walls are made of two layers of white exposed concrete. The wooden works in the part of the walls, roof and structure of the building are made of spruce or hand-cut shingles, and a part of the basement floor is covered by a type of European larch soil.

The playing room and gym in a sensory interaction with the outside world

Woodworks in the walls, roof and structure of the building

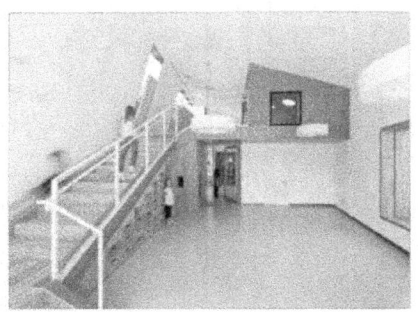

The stairs'space and the Locker room were filled with the light of day

Spaces which are bridged into the gallery and outdoor space

Figure 3.45. Kindergarten interior spaces

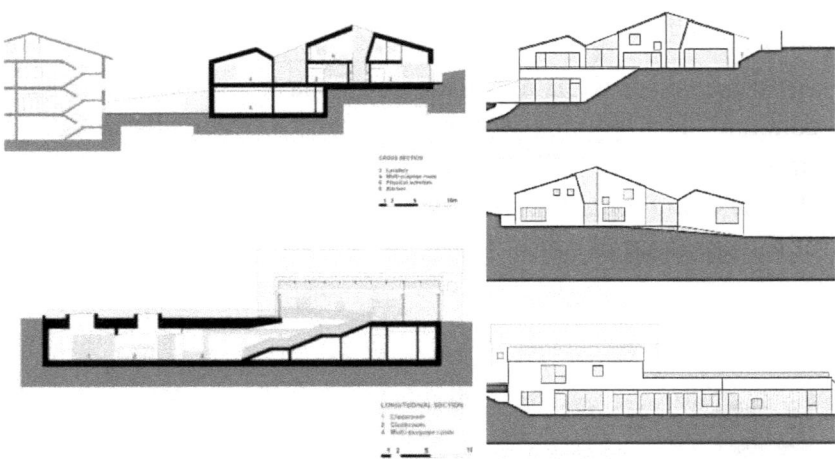

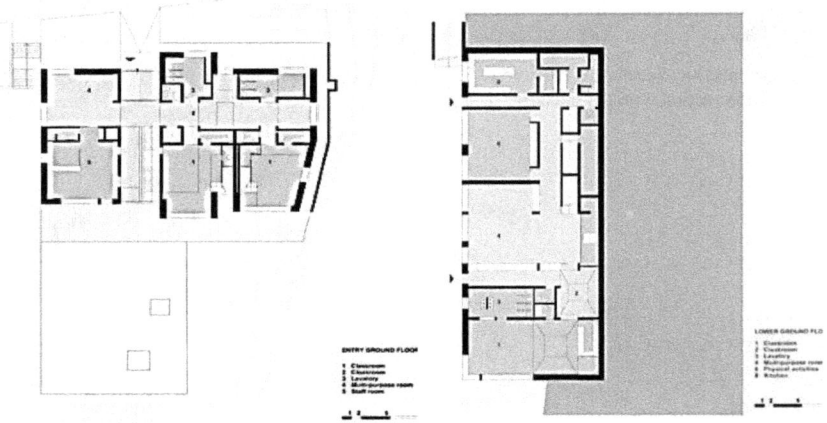

Figure 3.46. Facades and sections

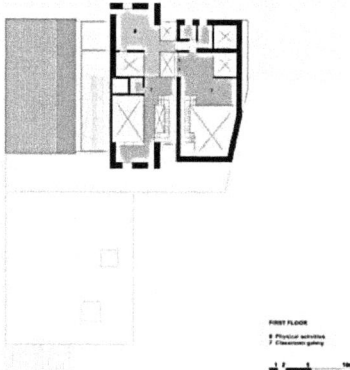

Figure 3.47. Trenten Kindergarten plans

- **A kindergarten in Chicago**

Figure 3.48. Building facade

The project located in the southern suburbs of Chicago includes a school for children aged between 3 months and 5 years old and a center where children can receive day care even after school hours.

This project was completed after the efforts of several institutions and non-profit organizations, especially the notable contributions of the Harris Charity Institute, the Chicago Public Schools Organization and the State of Illinois. This project develops more usable spaces for local children and provides an educational model for low-middle income communities.

Users and visitors of this project can clearly and easily understanding the design framework. The classes are organized on the sides of a square and the remaining middle courtyard serves as a large playground. Each wing contains a row of spaces with a classroom. The buildings are designed in different shapes and colors so that they are visually recognizable. Two corners of the square are used for access and the other two corners are left empty. Different rooms are connected to each other by an internal corridor having doors and openings to the exterior space. Since children's play spaces are very important, the courtyards that are directly accessible from the classrooms are positioned along the outer walls. Both the indoor and outdoor playgrounds account for the safety and security of children. Proximity to the highways and neighborhood apartments required a careful study of the security and privacy, and hence, the boundaries of the entire complex have been fenced. The materials have been selected with due consideration. The interior white plaster contrasts with the exterior painted wooden walls. In some parts, the wooden furniture is covered by upholsteries with original and bright colors in order to make it more familiar to children. The kindergarten is located in one of the poor areas of Chicago, close to the industrial area. Due to the unpleasant surroundings, the rooms are arranged around a central courtyard.

The main entrance of the kindergarten is located in one of the corners of the square. A small building that leads to a large room serves as a waiting space for parents who have come to pick up their children. A large ceiling skylight is installed in this space, which provides plenty of natural light.

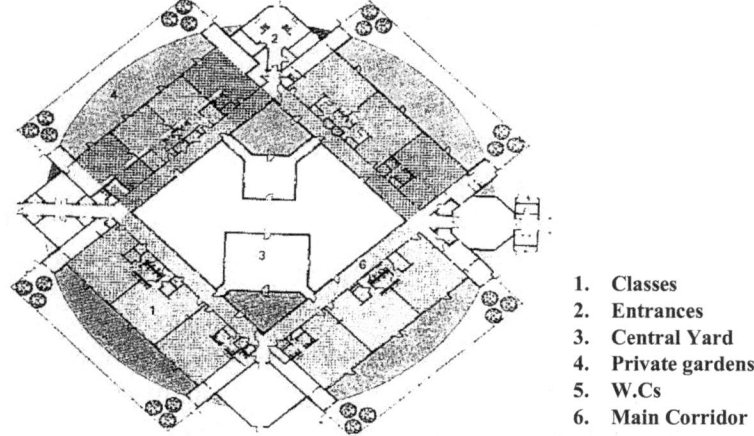

Figure 3.49. Chicago kindergarten plan

The courtyard is equipped with the equipment that has been designed to strengthen children's motor skills, without any sharp edges or screws that can hurt children. This equipment has strong bodies that make them resistant to wearing and tearing. Since classrooms are places where children spend most of their time, the architects and parents decided that their arrangement should be a special combination of group type. On the one side, the classrooms open to small private gardens, and on the other side, there is an interior glass corridor that leads to the central courtyard.

3.2 Conclusion

It should be acknowledged that in the examples reviewed, designers, in addition to responding to the specific needs and limitations of each project, try to establish a relationship between the architecture and children by considering factors such as space, color, light, gender, as well as respecting children' mental-psychological scale (through creating spaces with an intimate, familiar and understandable scale for them), and to this end, they presented various solutions.

Their design has been made considering children's flexible spirit, mental needs, and sensory and behavioral perceptions, as they are influenced by their surroundings. Stimulation of children's creativity by architectural elements should be regarded as one of the most obvious features of kindergarten design. In this way, the spaces reviewed have been designed in such a way that they stimulate children's mobility and dynamism.

Considering the fact that kindergarten spaces are designed and built for children, they must have at least a number of basic spatial characteristics for this purpose, including:

1. Paying attention to the principles of architecture and urban planning in kindergarten location.
2. Safety of the building for children.
3. Communication between the interior and exterior spaces.
4. Taking advantage of the maximum natural light of the day.
5. Creating a visual vision with the surrounding environment.
6. Appropriate use of colors according to children's mood. Using colors in designing the inner surfaces and even the outer surfaces of the classrooms can increase the desirability of the space for children.
7. Playing outdoors is considered as one of the important activities for children in a kindergarten, so it is necessary to consider one or more open spaces or yards for this purpose.
8. The use of innovative forms for the building with some of its elements such as doors and windows can increase the attractiveness of the building and distinguish it from houses and other architectural spaces.

9. Children's need to contact with nature and its elements, such as trees, flowers, and bushes, makes it necessary to use gardens and green spaces in kindergartens. Evaluation of the above examples indicates that different ideas can be used in this type of spaces, e.g., central courtyard, side courtyard, and strip green spaces.
10. Application of fluid and dynamic forms on floors and ceilings in order to encourage children to move and strive.
11. Application of soft lines and materials in the interior architecture of spaces.
12. Creating forms to stimulate children's imagination and discovery.
13. Observance of human sizes by considering the age group of children in order to keep establish psychological security of children.
14. Paying attention to hygiene, peace and sense of unity in children by creating a happy and fun environment using architectural elements.
15. Children in these kindergartens can engage in imagination, play, and social interaction, strengthen the sense of curiosity and feel the change in the seasons in connection with nature.

The important point is that the above principles should be observed in the best way.

3.3 Standards and Criteria for Kindergarten Architecture Design

3.3.1 Interior Space Design Criteria

3.3.1.1 Main Sections

The main section in a kindergarten include the administrative department, children's departments in two age groups, i.e., toddlers and newborns, communication spaces, multi-purpose hall, service and installations departments.

3.3.1.2 General Requirements

- The number of air switching in the kindergarten is twice an hour.
- The lower limit of indoor temperature is 20 C^0 in relative humidity of 30-80%.
- The upper limit of indoor temperature ranges between 25-27 C^0 respectively in relative humidity of 70-20%.
- Child departments should be separated from administrative and public spaces.
- The minimum height of the ceiling allowed for rooms with a depth of 6 to 8 meters is 3.25 meters, and for rooms with a smaller depth, 2.70 meters. When necessary, 25% of these spaces can have a height less than 2.10 meters. The minimum height for sanitary spaces is 10.2 meters.
- Floor coverings should be washable, disinfectable, and non-slippery.
- The covering of walls and columns should not be rough.
- There should not be any sharp parts on the surfaces of walls, columns and other elements.

3.3.2 Administrative Department

The administrative sector includes waiting space, office space, and reception space.

3.3.2.1 Waiting Space

Waiting space is the place of delivery and discharge of children and conversation between adults. The necessary equipment for this space includes notice boards, places for sitting, and water coolers. The minimum required area for the waiting area is 0.1 m² for each child.

3.3.2.2 Office Space

The office space includes different sections as follows:

- Space for the manager.
- Mailroom.
- Archive.
- Toilet and washroom.

In this space, necessary equipment including wardrobe, shelf, table, chair and sofa should be considered for different sections. The minimum area required in this section is 0.5 m² per child.

3.3.3 Children's block

Children's departments include the space assigned to keeping, playing and teaching children in two age groups, i.e., toddlers and newborns.

3.3.3.1 Toddlers' block

- This space is a place to care for toddlers and contains: dressing room, water closet, play, sleeping and sanitary areas.

- The minimum area required is 3.5^2 per toddler.
- The maximum number of children allowed in each toddler space is 15.
- The dressing room should be located at the entrance of the space and have an open shelf for the number of children and a tall mirror installed in safe conditions.
- The play space should be designed next to the child sleeping and resting space and in proper connection with it. The equipment needed in the open space includes: open and closed shelves. The minimum area required for the play space is 1 m² per toddler.
- The sleeping space should be equipped with a bed or mattress for the number of children and a shelf with a door. The minimum sleeping area for each bed is 1.4 m².

3.3.3.2 Young Children block

- This place is designed to care young children and includes: dressing room, training rooms, individual activities, library, art, education of a child, dollhouse, and sanitary space.
- The minimum area required for each child is 2 m².
- The dressing room should be located at the entrance of the space and have an open shelf for the number of children and a tall mirror installed in a safe manner.
- The training space should have direct access to the outdoor space as much as possible. Its equipment includes a trainer's table and chair, an open shelf, a table and a chair for the number of children. The maximum allowed number of children in each training room is 20 people and the minimum allowed area is 1 m² per child.
- The space for individual activities is a place for individual plays such as playing with building toys,

including: colored cubes, geometric shapes, wooden nails, etc. This space should be far from the commuting route. The equipment of this space includes: an open shelf, a table, and a child chair.
- The library space is a place for reading books and pictures. This space should be a quiet place and away from the training rooms and the art space. The equipment of this space includes: a notice board, a location for a number of books, a trainer's chair and a number of child chairs.
- The art space is a place for artistic activities such as: painting, pottery, playdough making, etc. This space should be away from high traffic areas. The equipment of this space includes: an open shelf with a door, a toilet bowl, a painting display panel, a child table and chair.
- A child training space is an enclosed space with equipment including: a table and a chair for a child and a trainer.
- A dollhouse is a place for children's imaginative play, playing with various home appliances that are prepared in small and portable sizes for children, such as telephones, brooms, kitchen appliances, sleeping appliances, etc. This space is equipped with an open shelf.
- For each training room, at least one sanitary space is required and this space must have the following conditions:
  - It should be located in a place where there is an easy and suitable access to it from the playground and the training rooms.
  - It should be equipped with two toilets, two wash basins and a closed shelf.
  - Its area should be at least 6 m^2.
  - Its entrance doors should be opened to the outside.

- The walls separating the toilets should have a maximum height of 140 cm.
- The walls should be tiled up to the ceiling and the separators should be made of washable materials.
- Its floor should be washable, durable and non-slippery.
- Electrical switches should be installed outside the sanitary area.

3.3.4 Shared Spaces

3.3.4.1 Multi-Purpose Hall

This space is used for different activities, holding ceremonies, gatherings for various occasions, and setting up an exhibition of children's artistic activities.

- This space is equipped with seats for at least 176 children. The minimum allowed area of this space for each child is 0.75 m^2.
- The corridors establish communication between spaces located on the same level.
- The corridors should have sufficient guidance signs and its different parts should be represented by using visual signs.
- The doors that open into the corridor should not be placed in such a way as to create an obstacle in the commuting path.

3.3.4.2 Staircase

The staircase connects the spaces located on different levels.

- The staircase path must be clearly marked with some kind of sign.

- The minimum height of the staircase ceiling (vertical distance between the edge of the staircase and the ceiling line) is 200 cm (Figure 3.50).

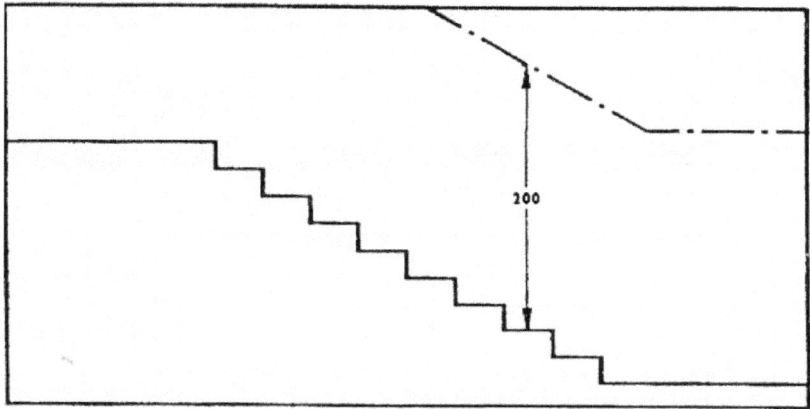

Figure 3.50. Minimum height of staircase ceiling

• The width of the staircase need to be at least 120 cm.

• The height of the staircase and the width of the staircase floor for children should be 12-15 cm and 27-33 cm, respectively.

3.3.5 Installation and Service Spaces

The service spaces include kitchen and storage, and the installation spaces include engine room and wall heater.

3.3.5.1 Kitchen

- The kitchen is a place to prepare raw materials and cook food.
- The kitchen should have a suitable space for preparing ingredients, cooking food and distributing it, washing utensils, storing ingredients, and cleaning tools.
- The location of the kitchen and its entrance should be chosen in such a way that there is minimal interference between its staff and other sectors of the kindergarten.

- The minimum area required for the kitchen should be 0.5 m² for each newborn child. The total area of the kitchen should not be less than 10 m².

3.3.5.2 Warehouse

- The warehouse is a place for storage of the additional kindergarten supplies and building maintenance items, e.g., cleaning materials, cleaning equipment, etc.
- The minimum area of the warehouse is 5.7 m².

3.3.5.3 Engine Room

- The engine room should be located in the basement or private yard.
- The required area for the engine room should be 0.02 times of the entire building infrastructure and at least 3×4 m in size.

3.3.6 Playground

- When designing the kindergarten playground, the climatic conditions of the place should be taken into account. In areas with very cold climate, the problems should be reduced by measures such as using wooden elements or plastic covers.
- In this type of climate, the slides should be facing the south in order to absorb the maximum sunlight.
- In hot climate, the arrangement of play equipment should be in such a way that the shade is used as much as possible. In this type of climate, the slides should be facing the north, so as not to be exposed to direct sunlight.
- In designing the playground, there must be suitable places for sitting. The elements of the space should be

considered in proportion to children's sizes (picture 50-4).

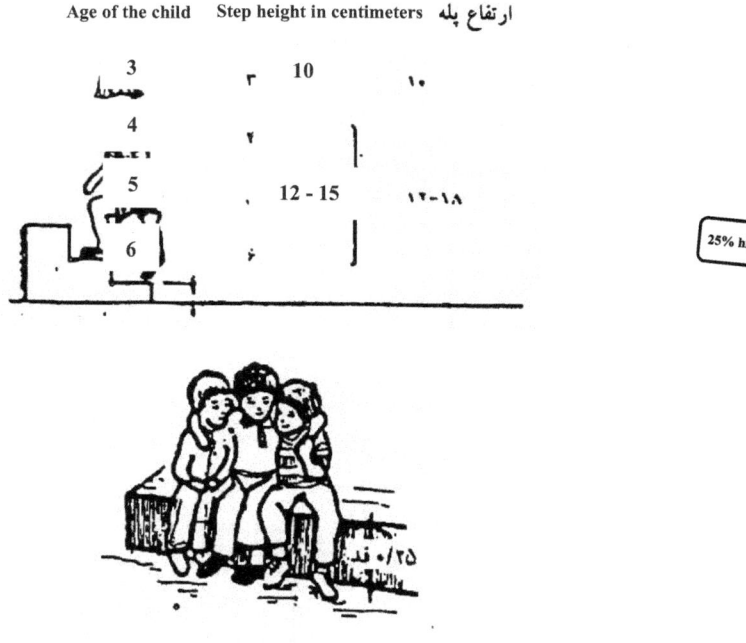

Figure 3.51. Seats and staircase suitable for children's sizes

- The covering of passageways and paths related to wheeled toys can be made of hard surfaces, such as concrete, stone, etc.
- Grass covering should be used for the surfaces between the play equipment.

3.3.7 Play Equipment

The prevalent types of child play equipment in kindergartens include: Carousel, slide, swing, climbing frame, and sandbox.

3.3.7.1 Merry-Go-Around

- The minimum land area required for the merry-go-around and its sanctuary is a circle with a radius of 300 cm.

3.3.7.2 Slide

- The minimum land area required for a slide and its sanctuary is 245×750 cm.

3.3.7.3 Swing

- The minimum area required for the swing and its sanctuary is 510×620 cm.

3.3.7.4 Climbing frame

- The minimum area required for the climber is 285×670 cm.
- The safe distance from the climbers on each side is at least 120 cm.

3.3.8 Suggestions

- In the kindergarten playground, the necessary facilities for various types of plays and for various activities (e.g., climbing, sliding, crawling, turning, swinging, playing with sand, sitting, etc.) should be considered.
- Toddlers' play should be separated from newborn children's play so that there is no possibility of collision.

3.3.9 Criteria for Adapting Existing Buildings

3.3.9.1 Criteria for Adaptation of Interior Spaces

- The minimum area per toddler can be considered 3.5 m^2.
- The minimum area per newborn child can be considered 1.5 m^2.
- The minimum capacity of the multi-purpose hall can be 40 children and the minimum storage area of this space can be considered 7 m^2.
- The kitchen area can be considered at least 10 m^2.

3.3.10 The Criteria for the Optimization of Open Space and Grounds

The minimum surface area for each child playing at a single time can be considered 2.5 m2. The area of the playground should not be less than 50 m2 in any condition.

Chapter 4.
Designing Children's Creative Space

4.1 Climatic Studies

4.1.1 Geographical Characteristics of Tehran

The geographic latitude of Tehran is 35 degrees north and its longitude is 51 degrees east. The height of Tehran is 1080 m above sea level. The summer temperature is 36 degrees and 48 minutes in summer and the winter temperature is 5 degrees and 52 minutes. The results of climatic studies and the general survey of Tehran climate indicates that this city has hot and relatively dry summers and cold winters.

4.1.2 Natural Geographical Location of the Site

The target site is located in the northern part of the physical structure of Tehran. Tehran itself is located in the southern slopes of the Alborz highlands and in the northern margin of the central desert of Iran, in a relatively wide plain. This area of the site is located in District 2 of Tehran Municipality.

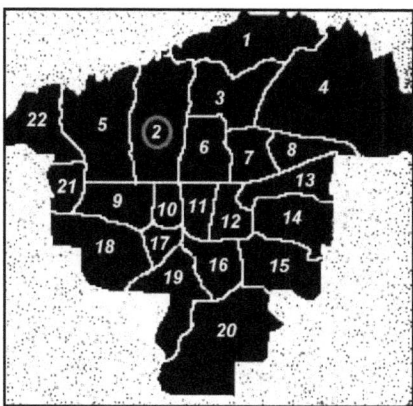

Figure 4.52 Site location

4.1.3 Climatic Features

Due to its special geographical location, Tehran has a completely different climate throughout the year, and given the dimensions and size of the area of this city, its climate survey cannot be explained in a statistical collection. Therefore, Tehran has been divided into five climatic zones for meteorological studies, and its 15-year statistics have been studied.

In summary, Tehran has hot and relatively dry summers and cold winters, but in terms of intensity and durability, its cold conditions are more than hot ones, and it is better in dealing with cold weather. The summers of these areas are mild and the winters are cold. Inside this area, moving towards the heights and increasing the height, the weather becomes colder. The precipitation rate is high and the freezing period is long. The winter cold continues until the beginning of spring, and after a mild period with cool nights, autumn arrives. In the atmosphere of early cold and short days in autumn, the presence of cold becomes more tangible.

4.1.3.1 Temperature

According to the results of the 15-year statistics (1981-1966) of the station, the average daily temperature in this station and consequently in the northern area of Tehran ranges between 22.5-27.5 C^0 and 0.7-6.9 C in the cold season and in the hot season, respectively. The average maximum and minimum temperatures are 35.7 C^0 and -7.5 C^0, respectively. The absolute maximum and minimum temperatures are 39 C^0 and 13.5 C^0, respectively. The results from the weather conditions of this station indicate that the weather in the northern part of Tehran is good in the summer and very cold in the winter, and the temperature difference from the center of the city reaches about 4 C^0.

4.1.3.2 Relative Humidity

The average maximum relative humidity ranges between 76 to 79%, which occurs in November and December. The minimum relative humidity ranges between 40 to 43%, which occurs in July, August, and September. The average daily relative humidity in this area is 47%. Considering the relationship between humidity and temperature, it can be concluded that in the cold months, the north of the city has sufficient humidity, and in the hot season, the air humidity decreases to an appropriate level.

4.1.3.3 Rainfall Rate and Number of Rainy Days

The results obtained from the rainfall statistics in the north of Tehran indicate that the average annual precipitation rate is 410 mm – the absolute maximum recorded in one month in the period under review is 185 mm and the average maximum is 820 mm (occurred in April). The monthly average minimum precipitation rate ranges between 1.4 to 5.6 mm, which occurs in July, August and September. It has been reported that the number of rainy days on the days when the precipitation rate is greater than 1 mm is 57 days during the year, and the number of freezing days is 73, the most of which has occurred in January followed by February and December. Also, there is no freezing in the period from April to November.

4.1.3.4 Freezing Days

The statistics of freezing days at this station indicates that an average of 20 freezing days has occurred in February. An annual average of 50 freezing days has occurred in this area. In this statistical period, freezing occurs in the period from November to April.

4.1.3.5 Snowy Days

In this period, there was no snowy days in this area only in 1966. The maximum number of snowy days during the year is 24 in January and February and 15 in September and October. On average, it snows 160 days a year in Tehran.

4.1.3.6 Wind

Among the 12 months, on average, December, January, and February are the calmest months in terms of wind, and the highest rate of wind occurs in April. In general, the wind speed that blows in Tehran throughout the year does not exceed 16 km/h, and this is the reason for the lack of favorable winds in hot days. As a result, the cool air with draught should be supplied by cooling systems inside spaces and places. The highest wind speed is 18 km/h from the west.

In Tehran, unfavorable winds blow from the southeast and south in spring and summer, and disturbing winds blow from the west and southwest in winter. If the educational environment is exposed to strong winds, the possibility of creating a green space by trees and bushes should be provided.

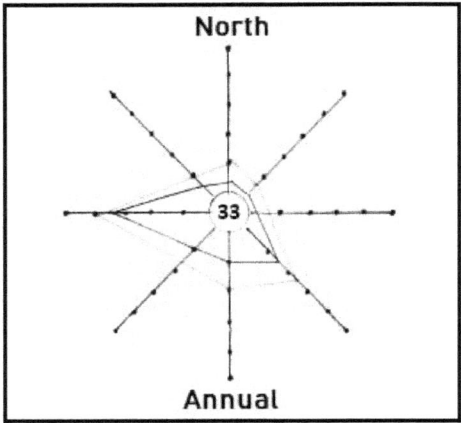

Figure 4.53 Wind

4.1.3.7 Sunlight

The angle of sunlight reaches at least 30 degrees on the first of December and reaches a maximum of 78 degrees on the first of July. In the hottest time of the year, the time when the sun is visible in the sky is from 5 am to 7 pm, and in the coldest time of the year, it is 7:30 am to 4:45 pm. The length of the shadow of a southern wall with a height of 1 m will be 1.73 m on the first of January (the shortest shadow) and 21 cm on the first of July (the longest shadow). To determine the direction of the building and pay attention to the hot and cold weather of the year, the state that absorbs the least amount of heat in summer and the most amount of solar energy in winter should be considered.

To this end, the building should be turned to the east by 45 degrees along the south. The radiation energy on the vertical surfaces of the building should be the most in winter and the least in summer. In order to gain maximum energy by the walls, the building should have a deviation of 22.5 degrees to the east. In this case, the southern front of the building will start receiving solar energy from 7:30 am in winter. This energy reaches its maximum value at 3:30 pm. At around 4 pm, all the energy gained is lost. At this hour, the western front of the building will have the maximum amount of energy received from the sun. In the hot season, the eastern and western exterior walls of the building will gain the most energy. This problem can be avoided by positioning the buildings next to each other.

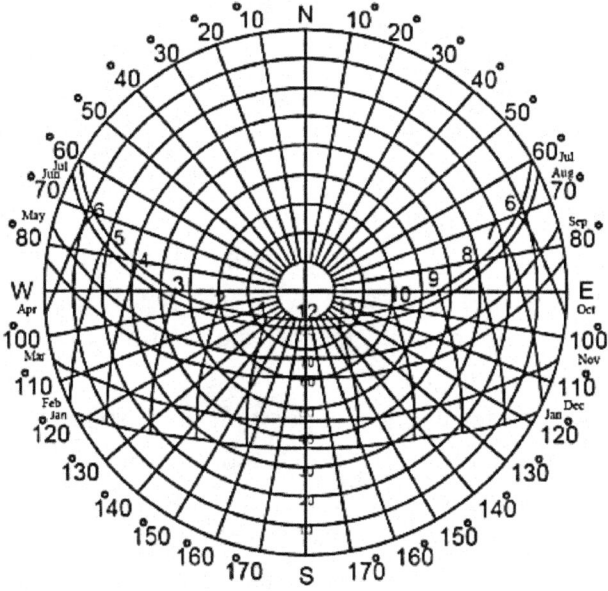

Figure 4.54 Sunlight

4.2 Site

4.2.1 Environmental Criteria for Kindergarten Location

The suitable place for the establishment of urban activities is primarily determined in urban development plans. The right place to establish a kindergarten should be chosen by observing

3 basic principles, i.e., user compatibility, location desirability, and capacity.

1. The site determined for the kindergarten location should have comfort, safety, and health conditions for the users. The users adjacent to the kindergarten should not have noise, environmental and air pollution. The most important users compatible with kindergartens include residential spaces, parks and green spaces, and cultural-recreational events.
2. Kindergarten location should be chosen in such a way that it has the least slope and unevenness in the desired place, according to the place topography.
3. The way of establishing the building in connection with the air flow should be in such a way that the effect of the disturbing winds is reduced and the intake of suitable and favorable winds is possible, so that the movement of air inside the building and natural ventilation is possible.
4. Kindergarten building position in respect to sunlight should be established in such a way that sunlight in winter and summer in its spaces is optimally suited to the climatic conditions of the place.
5. The kindergarten location in terms of the direction and angle of its radiation should be such that the spaces have proper light.
6. Kindergarten building should be built in a place where emergency vehicles such as ambulances and fire trucks can easily access it.
7. Entering the kindergarten should be possible without direct connection with the main streets, intersections, and squares.

According to the above, the site intended for designing a creative space for children is a land with an area of 42,650 m, which leads to the green space from both the south and west sides, and there is Hassan Seif Street on the opposite east side.

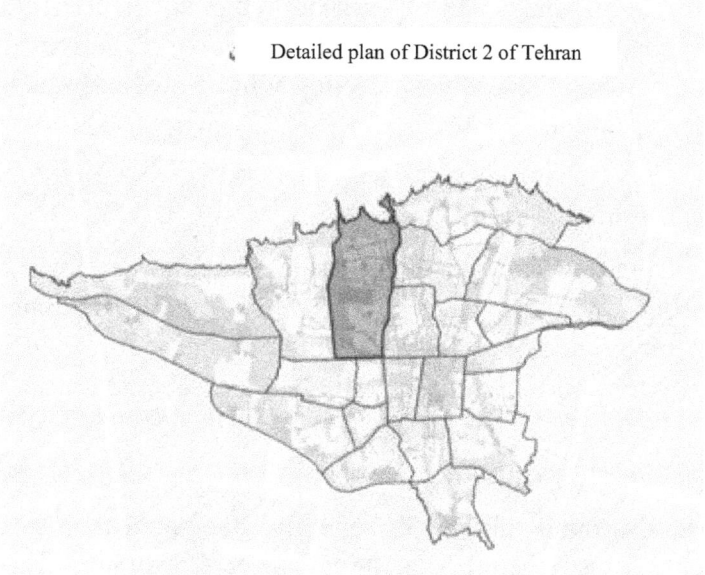

Figure 4.55 Detailed plan of the area

4.2.2 Site Analysis

The site considered for the kindergarten building is located in front of the 20th Alley on the west of Hassan Seif Street, District 2 of Tehran Municipality. In choosing the site to design a creative space for children, according to the available guidelines and criteria, an effort has been made to provide the maximum spatial criteria for the construction. The features of the site are mentioned below.

4.2.2.1 Construction Density and Physical Texture of the Neighborhood

The neighborhood that covers the site of this project has a relatively new texture in terms of architecture. The buildings around the site are mostly medium-sized and low-rise. One of its obvious features of the site is the absence of high-rise buildings in the vicinity of the site is. This is an important feature, as the existence of such buildings adversely influence the kindergarten circumstances in terms of negative effects such as creating shadows, affecting wind flow, and increasing the density of human traffic and vehicle traffic.

4.2.2.2 Vehicle Traffic

One of the key features of the project location is that it is far from highways and busy streets. This feature eliminates the problems related to noise, air pollution, and lack of sufficient security for children to pass through to a great extent.

4.2.2.3 Neighboring Uses

The land around the site is generally dedicated to residential uses, green space, and educational space. Considering the uses around the site, the neighbors are consistent with the educational space, and the proposed intended site does not have any problems in terms of its adjacent uses, and all the features that are suitable for educational use.

Figure 4.56 Municipality map (uses) of the site

4.2.2.4 Accesses

The site is located in a residential area, and there are no problematic commercial uses around it, so there is a low level of noise around the site. According to the maps related to the site analysis, the communication network around it is of the 1st grade type, with different levels of foot traffic, so it can be used optimally.

Figure 4.57 Accesses of the desired site

4.2.2.5 Checking the Entrances and Their Position on the Site

Since the site is located inside the city, it is necessary to comply with the urban development rules at the points of contact between the site and the outside complex. In this way, it is the first indicator of the entrances of the complex.

In the design of the complex, two types of entrances are considered:

1. Driver entrance
2. Pedestrian entrance

Chapter 4. Designing Children's Creative Space ➢ 147

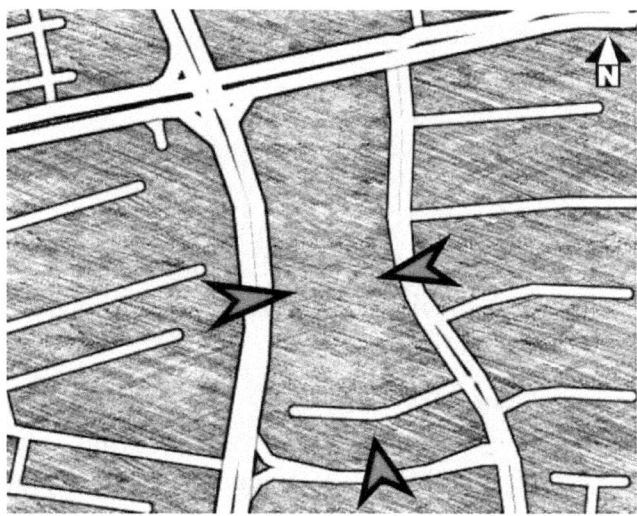

Figure 4.58 Entrances of the site

4.2.2.6 Noise Pollution

The site location is far from highways and busy streets. This feature eliminates the problem of noise pollution and air pollution to a large extent. In general, the proposed site can be exposed to noise pollution from the east side.

■ Main Spot of building
■ Noise
▨ Pollution free space

Figure 4.59 Noise pollution of the site

4.2.2.7 Climatic Conditions and Site

- **Wind**

In terms of neighbors with other buildings and geographical factors, the educational environment should be such that it is possible to move and ventilate the air. The way in which the educational building is established should be such that the effects of disturbing winds decreases and the availability of suitable winds increase.

In Tehran, unfavorable winds blow from the southeast and south in spring and summer, and disturbing winds blow from the west and southwest in winter. If the educational environment is exposed to strong winds, it should be made possible to create a green space by trees and bushes.

- **Sunlight**

The direction of educational buildings should be such that maximum sunlight is provided in the rooms during winter and penetration of disturbing radiation in summer is prevented.

Regarding radiation, the direction of 45 degrees southeast is proposed as the best direction. The examination of the wind direction and its effect on the building confirms this direction.

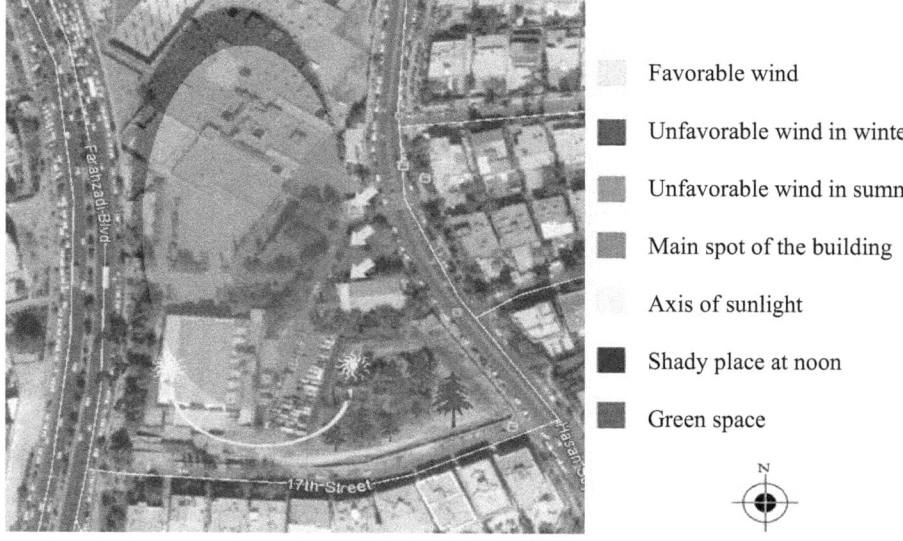

Figure 4.60 Climatic conditions of the site

4.3 Key points

A suitable place for construction of a kindergarten should include features of security, comfort, hygiene, and far from noise pollution. And also a park and green space can be constructed around the site. The kindergarten location should have the minimum slope and non-smoothness.

4.4 The Introduction of the Design Process

4.4.1 Compilation of Keywords in Designing

All humans have creative talent as children, but it cannot emerge due to lack of a proper environment and neglect and not strengthening this ability. This study is conducted to provide design ideas for special spaces for children with the approach of enhancing their creativity and examines the effect of diverse and flexible play spaces, nature, and green spaces on children's creativity.

4.4.2 Physical Program

The physical program is set up to build a creative space for children to accommodate a maximum of 200 children and is as follows, according to the user group:

- The toddler block: for a total of 70 toddlers (1.5 to 3 years old)

- The young children block: for a total of 130 young children (3 to 6 years old)

Table 4.1 Physical program

Row	The ground floor spaces	Unit area (m²)	Number	Total area (m²)
1	Kindergarten space			
1-1	Children's bedrooms	200	1	200
1-2	The teachers' rest area	90	1	90
1-3	W.C	2	5	10
1-4	Living room and Lobby	330	1	330
1-5	Dining hall	270	1	270
1-6	Food preparation	45	1	45
1-7	Food storage	50	1	50
	Indoor play			
1-8	Painting	88	1	88
1-9	dollhouse	88	1	88
1-10	Zoology	80	1	80
1-11	Colorology	80	1	80
1-12	Music	75	1	75
1-13	The story room	115	1	115
1-14	Aquarium and artificial beach	100	1	100
1-15	Swimming pool	90	1	90

Chapter 4. Designing Children's Creative Space ➢ 151

Row	The ground floor spaces	Unit area (m²)	Number	Total area (m²)
1-16	Multipurpose hall	110	1	110
1-17	Gallery	195	1	195
1-18	Research office	90	1	90
1-19	Stadium	400	1	400
2	Educational space			
2-1	Design training	150	1	150
2-2	Sculpture training	150	1	150
2-3	Computer training	85	1	85
2-4	Photography training	80	1	80
2-5	Pottery training	65	1	65
2-6	Collage training	80	1	80
2-7	Reading training	80	1	80
2-8	Handicraft training	90	1	90
2-9	language training	80	1	80
2-10	Rhythmic games training	80	1	80
2-11	Information and security	20	2	20
2-12	W.C	2	5	10
2-13	Store	20	1	20
2-14	Staircase Space	15	1	15
2-15	Research office	90	1	90
2-16	Living room and Lobby	180	1	180

Row	The ground floor spaces	Unit area (m²)	Number	Total area (m²)
3	Workshop space			
3-1	Construction workshop	145	1	145
3-2	Creativity workshop	105	1	105
3-3	Art workshop	175	1	175

3-4	Research workshop	120	1	120
3-5	Design workshop	105	1	105
3-6	Woodworking workshop	85	1	85
3-7	Materials workshop	90	1	90
3-8	Electrical workshop	80	1	80
3-9	Toy making workshop	85	1	85
3-10	Reading workshop	90	1	90
3-11	Drama workshop	115	1	115
3-12	Research office	90	1	90
3-13	Store	130	2	160
3-14	W.C	2	5	10
3-15	Staircase Space	15	1	15
3-16	Living room and Lobby	100	1	100
3-17	Information	10	1	10

4	Research space			
4-1	conference hall	155	1	155
4-2	Library	150	1	150
4-3	Library repository	35	1	35
4-4	Archive	35	1	35
4-5	Research office	90	1	90
4-6	Research	55	1	55
4-7	Training and skills	86	1	86
4-8	Children's participation in the design process	90	3	90
4-9	Creativity	90	1	90
4-10	Development and learning	100	1	100
4-11	Research block	100	1	100
4-12	Teaching parents	90	1	90
4-13	Communication with the child	90	1	90

Chapter 4. Designing Children's Creative Space ➤ 153

4-14	Teaching aids	85	1	85
4-15	W.C	2	3	6
4-16	Store	6	1	6
4-17	Staircase Space	15	1	15
4-18	Living room and Lobby	250	1	250
4-19	Information	10	1	10
The total area of the ground floor				6810 m²

Row	The first floor spaces	Unit area (m²)	Number	Total area (m²)
5	Administrative block			
5-1	Management	55	1	55
5-2	Secretary	28	1	28
5-3	Public relations and personnel	46	1	46
5-4	Conference and meeting rooms	80	1	80
5-5	Administrative Room	45	1	45
5-6	Secretariat	50	1	50
5-7	Archive	68	1	68
5-8	Parent-teacher interaction	40	1	40
5-9	W.C	2	3	6
5-10	Pantry	8	1	8
5-11	Information	10	1	10
5-12	The elevator room	4.5	2	9
5-13	Staircase Space	15	1	15
The total area of the First floor				460 m²

Row	The basement floor	Unit area	Number	Total area

	spaces	(m²)		(m²)
6	Installations	630	1	630
	Installations	450	1	450

Row	Amphitheater	Unit area (m²)	Number	Total area (m²)
7-1	Waiting area and exhibition	150	1	150
7-2	W.C	2	4	8
7-3	Backstage	110	1	110
7-4	Stage	105	1	105
7-5	Amphitheater space	430	1	430
7-6	Buffet	18	1	18
7-7	Information	18	1	18
7-8	Enter and exit	97	2	194
	The total area of the amphitheater			633 m²

4.5 The Design Process

Children's creative space is for children aged 2 to 6 years.

- The building is in the middle of the site and is designed in the form of a central courtyard due to the natural location of the site and its view of the surroundings. In this way, the visual connection between the interior and exterior space is maintained from all angles. The transparency and integrity of the internal and external spaces along with the presence of separating lines and borders make the space clear and legible.

- The entrance to the children's spaces should not be in direct contact with the street. So, it has been created via a pedestrian path and access from two streets adjacent to the project. It is an intermediate path between the child's creative space and the street. The entrance to the children's house is defined by the presence of nature and surrounded by trees.

- The space of the building is designed on one floor for maximum safety and comfort.
- The building is planned as open, semi-open, and closed spaces to meet the project's goals.

4.5.1 Open Spaces

The open space includes a central courtyard and a public courtyard. Most children's daily activities take place in the central courtyard, which has a playground, a space for children to jump and run, an amphitheater, a gazebo, and places to sit. The public yard has a basketball and tennis court for adults and a garden area, pond, green space, and a walking path for children.

An effective way to define or create a connection between different surfaces of a complex is to define the borders by flooring. For example, an area with special patterned flooring and certain materials will give identity to the spaces in front of it. Such flooring will also increase the variety and visual desirability of the environment. Open spaces have been tried to be defined by using surface differences, different elements and materials, including grass, wood, paving, granular flooring, and happy and lively colors that are the favorite of children and creating the diversity of space, view, and landscape.

Part of the open space design includes the paths where the children meet and the networks that connect the various spaces. Multiple side paths are recommended to be designed on the ground and branch off from the main path so that children can easily search and explore. Children learn through touch. They love soft textures (such as grass and carpet) and wood textures.

All children's senses can be considered with the diverse use of these textures in the building.

4.5.2 Enclosed Spaces

They include the child's creative space building, which consists of a kindergarten's part, educational, research, and administrative blocks, a workshop, and an amphitheater.

4.5.2.1 Kindergarten Classrooms

Kindergarten classrooms are designed for young children.

In these classrooms, all the furniture is designed according to the size of the children. They include painting, zoology, aquarium, artificial beach, and other classes.

A series of colored wooden beams that rotate on the central axis has created a happy, dynamic, and energetic view of the kindergarten's exterior. They constantly change the appearance of the kindergarten and affect the mood and education of children by entertaining children and playing along with teaching them colors.

4.5.2.2 Educational Classes

The educational classes are designed for different ages.

- Classroom furniture including tables and chairs suitable for children's sizes, boards, shelves, etc.
- There should be a place to store and place play equipment in the classroom so that children can easily take equipment from that place during free play and put it back regularly at the end of the play.
- Using the day's natural light and vision of the outdoors and nature, large windows create a pleasant environment.

- Green and blue colors are used in environments where considerable focus and vision are required.
- Spaces, where children can paint on the wall and floor, are designed.
- Elements such as doors, windows, and walls are designed to fit the size of the children so that they feel independent in their affairs.
- In these classes, activities such as sculpting, pottery, etc. are carried out.

Sports Hall

It is an indoor space used for sports such as gymnastics, yoga, etc. Children's sense of mobility is strengthened in this hall by using high height, color and form of windows, and lighting.

Multipurpose Hall

The multipurpose hall is a large space designed for children's group and individual activities. It is also a place for passing and social interactions between different age groups of children.

- Children like big spaces to do exciting activities and small spaces to be alone.
- Children's artwork is displayed in this space, and it should be flexible with changing functions.
- An extended view of the sky, nature, and open spaces is created for children by using windows in the walls and ceilings.
- A favorable, happy, diverse, and stimulating atmosphere is created for children by using colored glasses. They also prevent the glare of the daylight and control the light entering as desired.
- Children are encouraged to move by using fluid and dynamic forms on floors and ceilings.

- Children are happier and more excited in environments with happy and relaxing colors such as yellow and red. These colors are suitable for the color design in the playroom as a space for children's activities and encourage them to socialize.
- The use of soft lines and materials in the interior architecture of spaces
- The use of plants in the interior

4.5.2.3 Research Classes

Considering spaces for adults' use and research distinguishes this project from children's spaces. A library with full facilities has been considered for the research block so that it is not boring. Furthermore, a green roof is planned for this block for social relations and relaxation of adults, employees, and researchers.

4.5.2.4 Workshop Classes

In a workshop designed for children, an attempt has been made to create attractive, comfortable, and educational spaces for children, enabling them to participate in it theoretically and practically. Children's creativity will be enhanced by their participation in group work and by displaying their artwork. The blocks such as toy making, carpentry workshop, electrical workshop, etc. are considered in the workshop where children can participate under the supervision of teachers.

4.5.2.5 Amphitheatre

The distinguishing point of the project is the amphitheater, which is located in the center and is connected to all the blocks. A shell made of stretch metal is considered for this block. It can create an attractive view by being affected by the lighting.

4.5.2.6 Administrative Block

The administrative block has the following sections:

- Manager's office
- Secretary's room
- Office
- Secretariat
- Personnel department
- Archive
- Parent-teacher interaction
- Lobby

Services

- Canteen has three blocks, namely food preparation, food pantry, and dining hall. In the dining hall, a space simulated from the kitchen can be created according to the size of the children. It can promote children's imagination, independence, and comfort. This hall can also be a place for celebrating children's birthdays.

- In the children's rest area, an environment suitable for children is created by using similar colors for the child's rest and sleep area. Blue is very important in this space. It is the first and most important relaxing color that is useful for insomniacs due to its useful therapeutic properties such as nerve pain relief.

- A separate space is designed for the teachers to rest and overlooks the children's space.

- Besides, a lobby is designed for admission and discharge of children, waiting, and conversation between adults.

- An auditorium is intended for holding meetings, conferences, and parent training classes.
- W.C
- Installations
- Store
- Pantry

4.5.3 Semi-Open Spaces

All the blocks are designed to create spatial diversity in terms of form, color, lighting, materials, and functionality. Semi-open spaces are referred to indoor spaces, having one or two open sides, and directly connecting the outside space.

Wooden Cottages

Appropriate forms are tried to be used to achieve creative places and spaces. Since children have a deep relationship with nature, it has been tried to bring nature into the artificial space in addition to creating open environments where children interact with nature. Wooden huts are cozy spaces in connection with plants, as well as in connection with open air and natural light through a hatch installed on the roof. They are designed for storytelling classes, puppet shows, or free activities.

A green roof is intended for use by adults and diversification of the environment for the educational and research block.

4.5.4 Installations

The kindergarten is heated when needed by using the under floor heating system. This is the best method for such spaces. The movement of hot water is used in this system, in which the heat caused by the radiant energy of the sun can be benefited through the panels installed on the roof.

4.5.5 Structure

As mentioned in architectural planning, the building is a cultural, educational, and recreational complex with halls and workshops and has small, large, and medium spans. When studying a diverse complex from a structural point of view, side issues such as the possibility of constructing the building in terms of climate and technical skills, how to implement the project in terms of typology, types of structural systems, and economic issues of the project should be investigated in addition to structural issues that are important and worthy of investigation. The following should be considered the main factors of structural studies in addition to structural calculations.

1. It should be implemented as homogeneously as possible in terms of construction materials. For example, the uniform construction of the building in the form of concrete, metal, or wooden structures greatly affects the simplicity, uniform equipment of the workshop, and supervision of its construction.
2. The building should be made of relatively light materials. This will reduce the seismic force in addition to reducing the building weight.
3. The type of building and the materials used depend on the weather, wind, ambient temperature during the working season, and the importance of economic issues in terms of the speed of construction and the efficiency of buildings should be directly considered in choosing the kind of system.

4. Wind and earthquake forces, vertical forces, and their combined effects should be considered according to the climate and type of structure.

4.5.5.1 Concrete Frame System

This system is implemented as beam and column mold or in-situ concreting. The roofs are simultaneously concreted if they are made of concrete.

In this system, various forms can be created by using different molding. This system has advantages such as resistance to fire, ease of creating restrained joints, ease of implementation of shear walls, its continuity and integration with beam and column components, lack of rust unlike steel frame, and lack of vulnerability to fire. The post-tensioned concrete system is chosen for the complex to provide integrated spaces and large spans. The CCL post-tensioned concrete system is in harmony with the requirements of the project in addition to the advantages of conventional concrete. The flexibility of the system makes the construction of the soft form of the building easier than the steel frame system.

4.5.5.2 The General Safety of Glasses

A glass roof or canopy must meet many functional requirements, some of which are as follows.

- Visual functions: entry of daylight, visibility to the outside and the sky, appearance
- Thermal functions: heat loss, heat gain, thermal equilibrium
- Mechanical functions: glass useful life, glass strength, wind and snow loads, thermal stress, human impact, etc.
- Other functions: fire resistance and soundproofing.

4.5.5.3 Safety Requirements

Safety is the first functional requirement to be considered and an important issue in glasswork for levels above human height. There are two factors in this regard:

1. Selection of the type of glass and its characteristics
2. The design of the retaining system

The best usage for this cover is neither glass nor plastic alone, but a combination of them, the ability of each of which complements the weaknesses of the other. There are two main types of glass-plastic composites.

Laminated glass is usually made up of two layers of glass sandwiched together with an interlayer of plastic such as polyvinyl butyric (PVB), which provides greater structural safety than any single glass. Bonded composite units provide higher u-values than all glass products.

Retaining System

The most important retaining systems are the framed system, plate/screw systems, surface systems, and support connection systems.

4.6 Design Process Diagrams

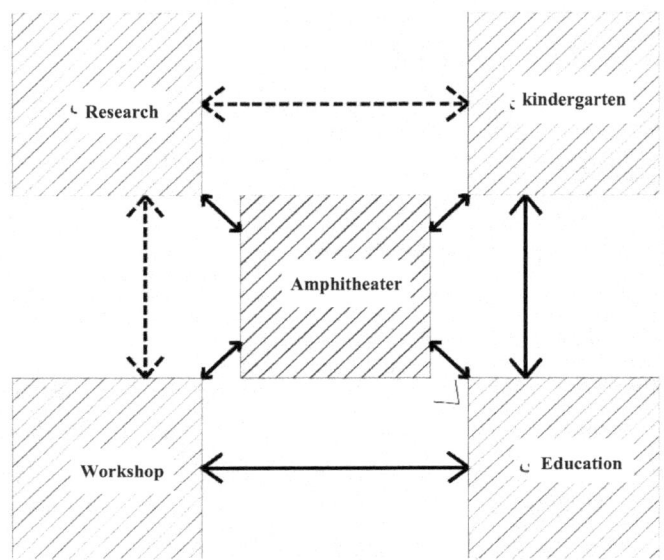

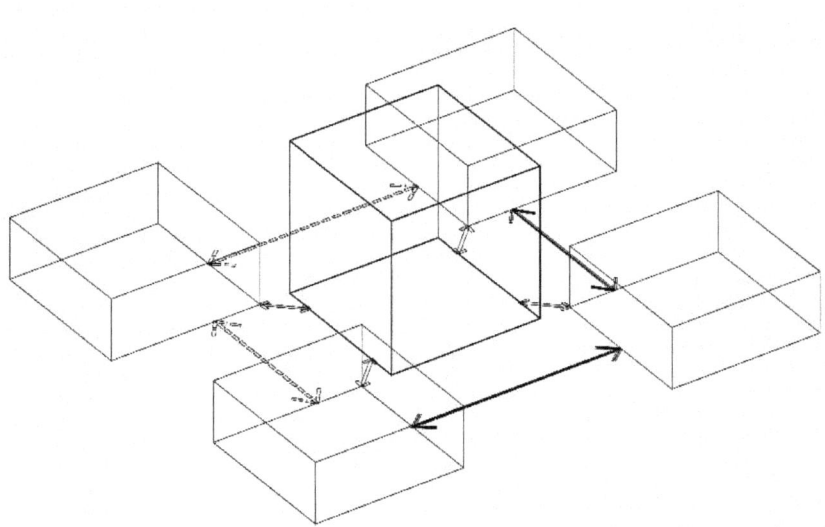

Figure 4.61 The diagram of Phase 1

Chapter 4. Designing Children's Creative Space ➢ 165

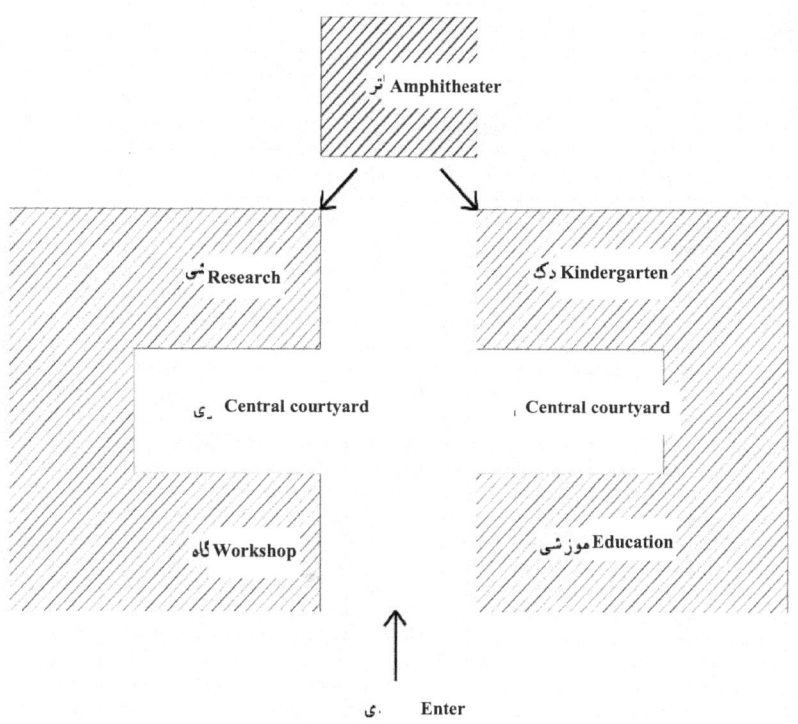

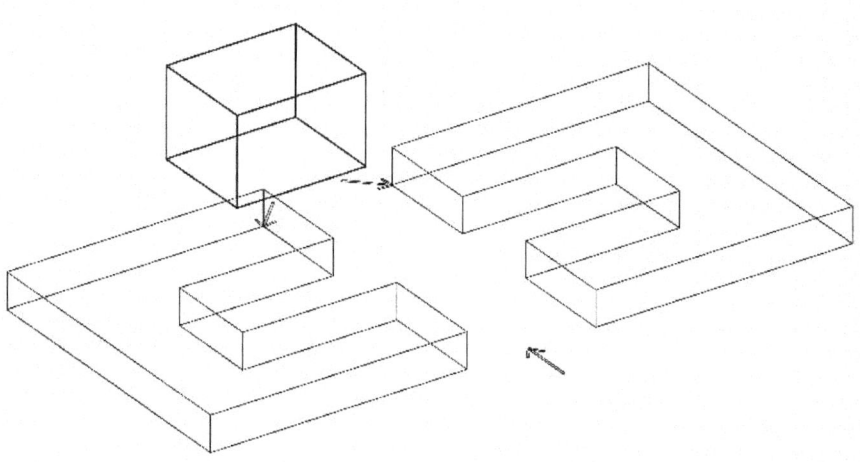

166 ◄ Designing Children's Creative Space

Figure 4.62 The diagram of Phase 2

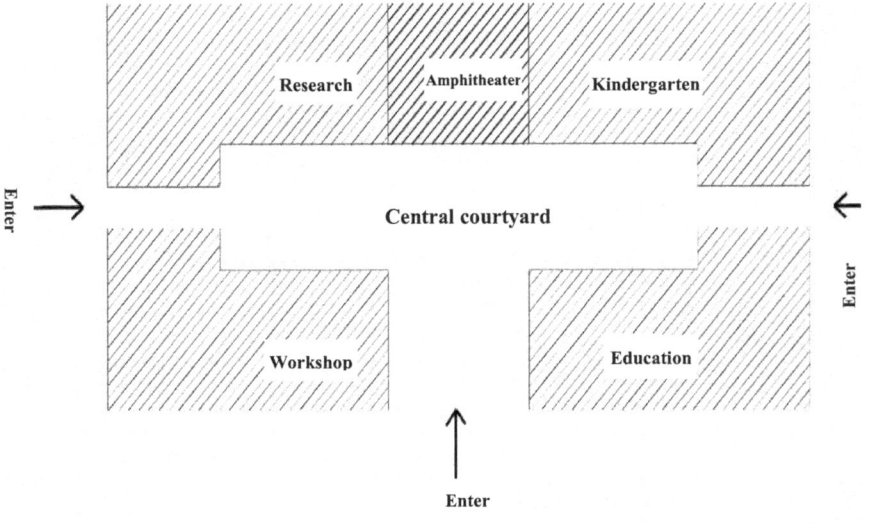

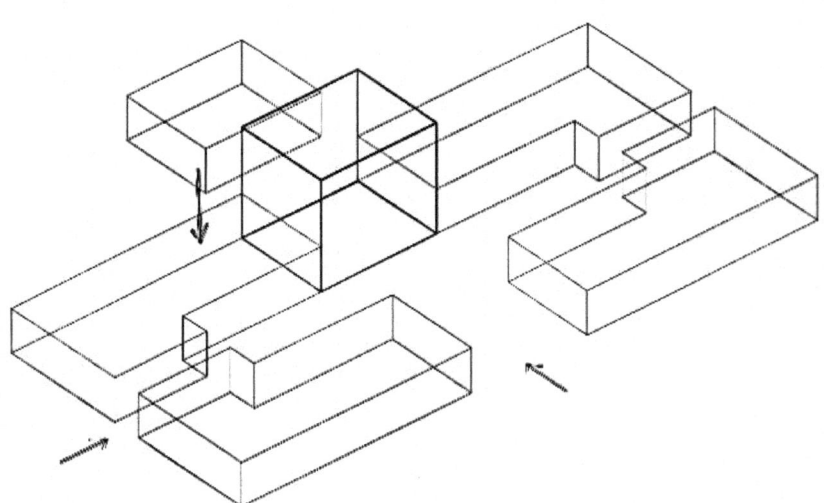

Figure 4.63 The diagram of Phase 3

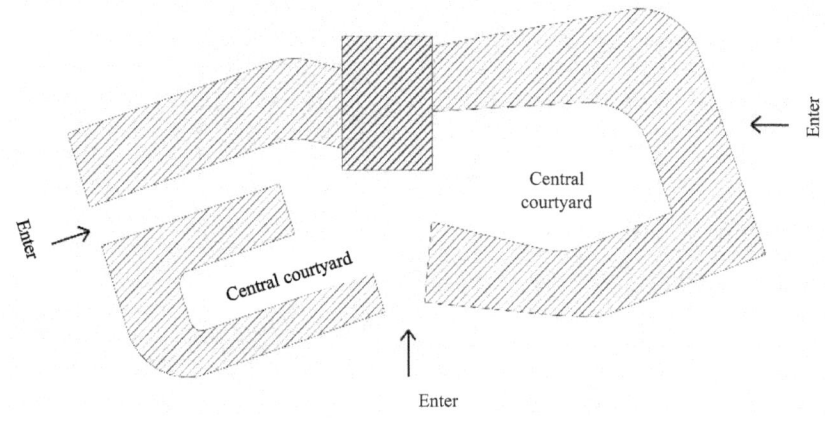

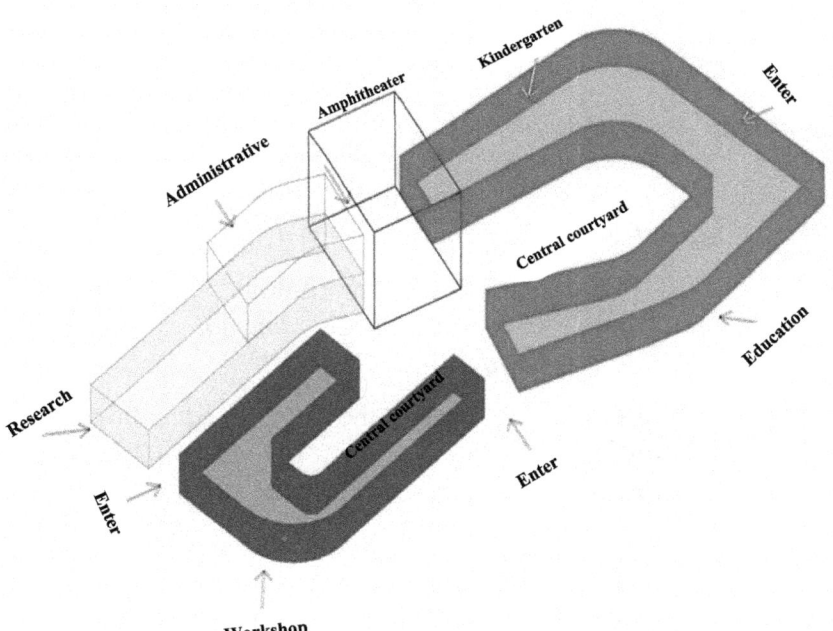

Figure 4.64 The diagram of Phase 4

References

Aghapour, M., Jamshidiha, Gh., Farrokhi, A. (2006). A meta-analysis of the interaction between motor and social development. *Journal of Harakt*, No. 27, 153-171.

Ahmadvand, M.A. (1994). *Play Psychology*, Tehran, Kayhan Publications.

Aiken, L.R. (1973). *Ability and creativity in mathematics.* Review of educational Research, 43(4), 405-432.

Alaedini, Z., Kalantari, M., Kajbaf, M., & Molavi, H. (2015). The Effectiveness of Role-Playing Games on Emotional And Cognitive Creativity Among Primary School Children. *Journal of Developmental Psychology: Iranian Psychologists*, 12(45), 15-25.

Aldous, C. R. (2007). Creativity, problem solving and innovative science: Insights from history, cognitive psychology and neuroscience. *International Education Journal*, 8(2), 176-186.

Amabile, T. M. (1983) Social psychology of creativity: A componential conceptualization. *Journal of personality and social psychology*, 45, 375-367.

Amin, A., Mahouzi, R. (2013) the role of education in the fertilization of creativity in children, *Journal of Philosophy and Theology*, 1(1), 15-26.

Amiri, A., Norouzi, D. (2011) Comparing the effectiveness of two methods (TRIZ and brainstorming) on the creativity of the E-learning training students of Khaje Nasir University, *Quarterly Journal of Innovation and Creativity in Human Sciences*, 1(4), 85-120.

Bahremand, H., Fallahchai, R. & Zarei, E. (2014). Relationship between self- esteem and creativity with prejudice in students. *Applied environmental and biological sciences*, 4 (1), 51-53.

Bayat, A.& Yaghoubi, A. (2014). The Relationship between Self-Esteem on Happiness and Creativity of Bu-Ali Sina University Students. *Quarterly Journal of Innovation and Creativity in Human Sciences*, 3(4), 147-164.

Behpajooh, A. (2010). What is creativity? Who is a creative child? *Payvand Journal*, No. 356, 8-11.

Bohm, David (2002). On Creativity, (Hossein Nejad, M, A. Trans). Tehran, Saghi Publications.

Boroon, S., Heidari, A. & Bakhtiarpour, S. (2014). The effect of creative problem-solving training on creative components on students, *Quarterly Journal of Innovation and Creativity in Human Sciences*, 2(8), 55-71.

Cheragh Cheshm, A. (2008). An investigation into the influence of creativity-based teaching methods on students' education and learning, *Byquarterly Journal of Islamic Education*, 3(5), 7-36.

Csikszentmihalyi, M. (1996). *Creativity: Flow and the psychology of discovery and invention.* New York: Harper/ Collins.

Davies, T. (2000). Confidence! It`s Role in the Creative Teaching and Learning of Design and Technology. *Journal of Technology Education*, 12(1), 18-31.

Delotaj Bakhsh, R. (1998). Master's Thesis in Architecture, Faculty of Art and Architecture, Islamic Azad University, Central Tehran Branch.

Druckman, D., & Bjork, R. A. (1994). Learning, remembering, believing: Enhancing human performance. Washington, DC: The National Academies Press. Erikson stages of psychosocial development. *Journal of Youth and Adolescence.*

Eysenck, M. W. (1979). Anxiety, learning, and memory: A reconceptualization. *Journal of Research in Personality.*

Eysenck, MW. (1994). *The Blackwell Dictionary of Cognitive Psychology*, (Kharazi, A. Dolati, R. Raisi, M. Kamali, GH & H. Trans). Ney Publication.

Firestien, R.L. (1996). *Leading on the Creative Edge: Gaining Competitive Advantage Through the Power of Creative Problem Solving.* Colorado Springs, CO: Pinion Press.

Gagne, R. (1985). *The Conditions of Learning* (4th Ed.). New York: Holt, Rinehart & Winston.

Geographical Climatic Survey of Tehran, (1998). Tehran Conservation and Planning Plan, Ministry of Roads and Urban Development Islamic Republic of Iran.

Glyn V, T., Silk, A. (1991). An introduction to the psychology of children's drawings, (Mokhber, A. Trans) Tarh -e-No Publications.

Gordon, W. J. J. (1961). *Synectics: The Development of Creative Capacity.* New York: Harper and row.

Gorzoldini, M. (2015). methods of developing painting creativity in elementary education, *Art and Architecture Magazine*, 12(39), 44-48.

Guilford.J.P.(1967). *The nature of human intelligence.* McGrahill. New York NY.

Hamza, M. K., & Griffith, K. G. (2006). Fostering Problem Solving & Creative Thinking in the Classroom: Cultivating a Creative Mind. *National forum of applied educational research journal- electronic*, 19(3), 1-31.

Heller, K. A. (2007). Scientific ability and creativity. High Ability Studies, 8(2), 209–234.

Jung, C. G. (1999). *Personality Development, first edition*, (Tavalaei, H. Trans). Tehran, Atiyeh Publications.

Kaedi, R.& Roumani, S. (2016). *The Role of Play in Children's Development.*

Kandemir, M. A., & Gur, H. (2007). Creativity Training in Problem Solving: A Model of Creativity in Mathematics Teacher Education. *New Horizons in Education*, 55(3), 107-122.

Kaprova, E., Marcketti, S. B., & Barker, J. (2011). The Efficacy of Teaching Creativity: Assessment of Student Creative Thinking before and after Exercises. *Clothing and Textiles Research Journal*, 29(1), 52-66.

Kasmai, M. (2003). *Climate and Architecture*, Khak Publications.

Kefayat, M. (1995). *Investigating the relationship of parenting styles and atttudes with creativity and the recent variable relationship with intelligence and academic progress of first-year students in Ahvaz boys' high schools*. Master's Thesis in Educational Psychology, Shahid Chamran University of Ahvaz.

Kefayat, M. (1995). *Investigating the relationship between parenting Styles and attitudes with creativity and investigating the relationship between creativity and intelligence and academic achievement*. Master's thesis. Supervisor Hossein Shokrkon. Faculty of Education and Psychology, Shahid Beheshti University.

Khodaei M, V. (2016). Evaluating the Psychological Methods of Teaching Self- confidence in Iranian Children's Stories. *Journal of Instruction and Evaluation*, 9 (33), 137-158.

Kim, Majd., Roh, I. S., & Cho, M. K. (2016). Creativity of Gifted Students in an Integrated Math-Science Instruction. *Thinking Skills and Creativity*, 19, 38-48.

Kindergarten Design Criteria, (2004). Ministry of Roads and Urban Development Islamic Republic of Iran, *Road, Housing & Urban Development Research Center*.

Kinga, S., Paul, M., & Stefan, S. (2015). Associations between Hexaco model of personality structure, motivational factors and self-reported creativity among architecture students. *Social and Behavioral Sciences*, 187, 130-135.

Kroner, W. (2006). *Architecture for Children.* (Khoshnevis, A. &Mir Rahmati, E. Trans). Ganj-e-Honar Publications.

Kroner, W. (2009). *Architecture for Children*, (Khoshnevis, A. Trans). Sayeh Gostar Publications.

Kuo, F., Chen, N., & Hwang, G. (2014). A creative thinking approach to enhancing the web-based problem solving performance of university students. *Computers and education*, 72, 220-230.

Lally, R., Stewar, J. (2005). Infant and Toddler Spaces, *American Academy of Pediatrics*, 2005.

Lüscher, M. (2010). *Luscher Color Test*, (Ebizadeh, V. Trans.) Tehran, Dorsa Publishing.

Mahmoudinezhad, H. (2014). *A compilation of the Urban public space designing criteria and principles for vulnerable groups* (children case study).

Makri, A., & Mylonas, K. (2009). Motor creativity and self-concept. *Creativity research journal*, 21(1), 104- 110.

Manteghi, M. (2012). Investigating the effect of creativity education on preschool and primary school students. *Journal of Curriculum Research (JCR)*, 2(1), 1-28.

Mokhtari, F. (1997). *The Psychology of Children's Painting.* Aghaghi Publications.

Mombini, Kh. (2001). *The relationship between creativity, self-fulfillment and self-esteem of male teachers with mental health, their job performance and academic performance of third to fifth grade students in Baghmalek primary schools*. Master's thesis in Educational Psychology, Shahid Chamran University, Ahvaz.

Moradi, A. & Rashidpour, A. (2014). The role of creativity in the process of solving cultural problems through cultural synergy. Quarterly *Journal of Cultural Engineering*, 8(78), 158-177.

Neufert, E. (2000). *Architects' Data*. (GohariNaini, M. Trans.) Tehran, Azarang Publications.

Osborn, A. F. (1957). *Applied imagination: Principles and procedures of creative problem solving*. New York: Charles Scribner's Sons.

Pakbin, M., *A Kindergarten in Gholhak*, Master's Thesis in Architecture, Faculty of Fine Arts, Tehran University.

Piaget, J.; Inhelder, B. (1989). *The Psychology of the Child*, (Tofigh, Z. Trans) Ney Publication.

Radbakhsh, N.; Mohammadifar, M. A, & KianErsi, F. (2013). Comparing the effectiveness of play and storytelling on increasing children's creativity. *Quarterly Journal of Innovation and Creativity in Human Sciences*, 2(4), 177-195.

Rogers, C. R. (1977). *Carl Rogers and humanistic education*. CH, Patterson, Foundations for a Theory of Instructional and Educational Psychology.

Shariatmadari, A. (1965). *Principles and Philosophy of Education*, Amirkabir Publications, Tehran, 44th edition.

Sharifi, A. A. & Davari, R. (2009). Comparison of the Effect of Three Methods of Creativity Development in Second Grade Guidance School Students. *Iranian Journal of Psychiatry and Clinical Psychology*, 15(1), 57-62.

Shokrkon, H.; Boroumandnasab, M.; Najarian, B. & Shehni Yeylagh, M., (2003). Examining Simple and Multiple Relationships of Creativity, Achievement Motivation and

Self-esteem with Entrepreneurship in Students of Shahid Chamran University. *Psychological Achievements*, 2(9), 1-24.

Shokrkon, H.; Brooomandnasab, M.; Najarian, B. & Shehni Yeylagh, M., (2003). Examining Simple and Multiple Relationships of Creativity, Achievement Motivation and Self-esteem with Entrepreneurship in Students of Shahid Chamran University. *Journal of Education and Psychology*, 2(9), 1-24.

Sobhi Gharamaleki, N. (1999). creativity and its cultivation methods in children, *Journal of Development of Educational Technology*, March 1999, 15 (6), 3-9.

Steiman, R. (2001). The importance of play in children's cognitive development and creativity. (Algheylipour Farzani, A. Trans) *Journal of Development of Educational Technology*, December 2001, 16 (4),7-8.

Stein, M.I. (1974). Stimulating creativity. New York: Academic Press.

Sternberg, R. J. (1988). The Nature of Creativity. New York:Cambridge university press.

Sternberg, R. J., & Davidson, JE. (1983), *Educational Psychologist*. Stryker, S. The keys to fostering children's artistic creativity (Gheitasi, A. Trans.) Daneh Publications.

Tabrizi, Gh. (1996). *An Introduction to Developmental Psychology*. Aydin Publications.

Taylor, A. J. W. (1966). Beatlemania: A Study in Adolescent Enthusiasm. *British Journal of Social & Clinical Psychology*.

Torabi, Z., Nazemi, M. *Application of environmental psychology knowledge in creative space design for children*, Islamic Azad University, Zanjan Branch.

Torrance, E. P. (1962). *Guiding Creative Talent*. Prentice-Hall, Inc.

Torrance, E. P. (1975). *Creativity research in education: Still alive*. In I. Taylor & J. Getzelz (Eds.), perspective in creativity. Chicago: Aldine.

Torrance, E.P. (1998). *An interview with E Paul Torrance: About creativity*. Educational psychology revives.

Woolfolk, A. E. (1987). *Educational psychology* (3rd ed.). Prentice-Hall, Inc.

Zare, H., Pirkhaefi, A.& Mobini, D. (2010). Effectiveness of Problem Solving Skills Training in Developing Engineers' Creativity with regard to Their Personality Types. *Journal of Modern Industrial/Organization Psychology*, 1(3), 49-56.

Zeinali, Z. (2010). *The relationship between metacognitive strategies and creativity with self-esteem and academic performance of high school students in Sedeh city*, Master's thesis, Faculty of Educational Sciences and Psychology, Marvdasht Branch.

Zera'at, Z. & Ghafourian, A. (2009). Effectiveness of problem solving skill teaching on students' educational self-thought. *Journal of Educational Strategies*, 2(1), 23-26.

www.ingramcontent.com/pod-product-compliance
Lightning Source LLC
Chambersburg PA
CBHW061731040426
42453CB00026B/627